» THE «

QUICK PICKLE

» COOKBOOK «

» THE «
» QUICK PICKLE «
» COOKBOOK «

RECIPES & TECHNIQUES FOR MAKING
& USING BRINED FRUITS & VEGETABLES

GRACE PARISI

QUARRY

Quarto is the authority on a wide range of topics.

Quarto educates, entertains and enriches the lives of our readers—enthusiasts and lovers of hands-on living.

www.QuartoKnows.com

First published in the United States of America in 2016 by
Quarry Books, an imprint of
Quarto Publishing Group USA Inc.
100 Cummings Center
Suite 406-L
Beverly, Massachusetts 01915-6101
Telephone: 978.282.9590
Fax: 978.283.2742
QuartoKnows.com
Visit our blogs at QuartoKnows.com

10 9 8 7 6 5 4 3 2 1

ISBN: 978-1-63159-144-0

Digital edition published in 2016
eISBN: 978-1-63159-205-8

Library of Congress Cataloging-in-Publication Data available

Cover and Book Design: Rita Sowins / Sowins Design
Photography: Glenn Scott Photography, except for pages 55, 62, 89, 102-103, 110, and 134 by Shutterstock

Printed in China

Contents

Vegetable Pickles

Fruit Pickles

PREFACE

When I was approached to write this book, my initial thought was, "Quick Pickles? *Really?* Sure, I like making pickles, but is there enough variety to fill a book? And, if so, how can I make *this* book different from every other pickle book out there?" Well, of course, upon greater consideration, I realized, yeah, there are a *ton* of pickles to fill a book. And, what sets *this* one apart from the rest is the discovery, along the way, of how pervasive pickles are in everyday cooking. This isn't merely a pack-your-cukes-into-a-jar-end-of-story kind of story. Rather, it's a how-to-showcase-all-those-delicious-pickles-that-you've-just-made kind of story—pickle juice included.

That's the story I wanted to tell. Here's one scenario: You've made a batch or two of awesome pickles, and maybe eaten a good portion of them. But there's about half a jar of stragglers and all that tangy pickle juice left. Do you toss it to make room for something else in your fridge? I certainly hope not. Chop some dill pickles and add them *and* some brine to a Russian Beef Barley Soup with Pickles called *Rassolnik* (pg 18). Or use half of your Fire-Roasted Pickled Baby Bells in an amazing Spanish *Romesco* sauce (pg 85). Or purée some Pickled Sweet Beets with Pearl Onions into a Super Quick Borscht (pg 36). These are just a few of the recipes that use pickles and their brine to create a completely new dish.

Then there are the myriad ways to use the pickles themselves: Cram some Pickled Red Cabbage with Horseradish and Caraway (pg 77) into an ooey gooey grilled cheese sandwich. Or serve Crunchy Pickled Pears (pg 127) with warm, baked Camembert. Or mash some Bourbon-Pickled Blackberries (pg 97) into whipped cream and crushed meringues for an awesome Eton mess.

One other thing I wanted to point out is that in these pickle recipes, the brine is as important as the produce. And, in many cases, the brine is the star of another, separate recipe. The Pineapple-Aperol Spritz (pg 136), for example, uses the tropical-flavored, sweet-tart brine as the base for a cocktail, and the pineapple itself is only a garnish. The brine alone from the Pickled Plums (pg 107) becomes a tart and refreshing granita (pg 108). Both totally unexpected and totally delicious. Unlike the *pickle-back* (a shot of pickle juice after a shot of whiskey) the pickles here aren't an afterthought, a side-attraction, or a dare. They're the main event—and the only dare is to make them and not love them. I hope you'll try to prove me wrong.

FOREWORD

I've written seventeen cookbooks. Some of my books have taken years to write, with extensive research and many recipes. Others are smaller, single-subject recipe books. My first book *From Tapas to Meze* was my firstborn and continues to hold me by the heartstrings. My most recent book, *Kitchen Gypsy: Recipes and Stories from a Lifelong Romance with Food* has been a pure passion project near and dear to my soul. And it's Grace Parisi I have to thank for bringing me into this most recent project.

Let me back up a little bit! I've known Grace for years. At first, it was her sound reputation I knew from her years working at *Food & Wine* magazine. Like everyone, I held her name with the highest regard. A few years later, I met Grace in person when we worked on a story together for the magazine. She was everything I'd heard—smart and talented.

I hadn't seen Grace for a while, and then a couple of years ago we sat together at an industry dinner in Chicago.

"You two should do a book together," Grace said as she generously introduced me to the editor-in-chief at Oxmoor House.

That's how *Kitchen Gypsy* began, and what transpired was magical. Grace and I worked closely on my book. She traveled to San Francisco several times to test recipes and style the recipes. As we worked side by side, I marveled at her creativity, patience, perseverance, and genuine congeniality.

What Grace brings to the table every time she jumps into a project is her intelligence, expertise, and passion. Take this book about pickles, for example. Reading the recipes will make you want to run into your kitchen and cook up a batch of Pickled Plum Tomatoes with Chipotle, Spicy Bread-and-Butter Pickles, or Lime-Chile Pickled Pineapple! And that's what a good cookbook is supposed to do, right?

JOANNE WEIR
Chef, teacher, television personality,
and James Beard Award–winning cookbook author

Salt: Some picklers insist on using pickling salt (pure sodium chloride) in their recipes because it doesn't contain additives such as potassium iodide, dextrose, and calcium silicate (an anti-caking agent which can sometimes make the brine cloudy). Pickling salt is not widely available and sometimes needs to be ordered online. The recipes in this book all use kosher salt, which is readily available and doesn't have additives. I like Diamond Crystal, and I tested the recipes with it.

Vinegar: Most commercial vinegars have acidity levels of 5 to 7 percent, which is perfect for pickling. For many of the recipes here, I've used distilled white vinegar. It's colorless and the flavor is neutral, so it doesn't compete with the aromatic spices and fruit and vegetables. I also like cider vinegar for pickling for its fruity flavor.

Some recipes call for balsamic vinegar and white balsamic vinegar. The flavor is lovely and perfectly *agro dolce* (sweet and sour). I call for regular balsamic for a darker brine and white balsamic for a lighter brine. It's purely visual. One thing, though, don't waste your money on an expensive, aged balsamic vinegar for pickling—it's better suited to finishing a dish. Red and white wine vinegars tend to be aged a bit and lend a bold and complex flavor.

Rice vinegar is mild and mellow, and at 3 percent acidity it's not acidic enough on its own to use as a pickling brine. If you want to use rice vinegar, you can use equal parts rice and distilled white vinegar to raise the acidity level.

Aromatics: Aromatics fall into two types—fresh herbs and dried spices. In both cases, larger is better. For fresh herbs such as dill, tarragon, basil, rosemary, thyme, bay leaves, oregano, kefir lime leaves, and lemongrass, whole sprigs or large leaves are better than chopped because they look pretty and are easy to pick around.

Spices, too, are better whole for a slightly different reason—ground spices make the brine look a bit murky. Some perennial pickling favorites are whole mustard seeds (yellow, brown, or black), coriander seeds, celery seeds, allspice berries, cloves, dill seeds, peppercorns, fennel seeds, caraway, dried red chiles, and whole cinnamon sticks. I also love fenugreek, nigella, cardamom, star anise, and saffron.

In several fruit pickle recipes I wanted a clear brine with lots of flavor but no aromatics to pick out. For those, I steeped whole spices in the brine then strained it into the jars.

Produce: Always look for the freshest fruits and vegetables—ripe but firm—with no blemishes or mold. Wash well. For cucumbers, kirbies are best but they are not always available year-round. If I'm jonesing for Killer Diller Pickles in the off-season, Persian cucumbers work pretty well. Be sure to trim a thin sliver from the ends of cucumbers. The blossoms contain enzymes that make the pickles especially soft if not removed.

Process

〚 EQUIPMENT 〛

Jars: Unless you plan to process your pickles for storing at room temperature, you can use any type of jar as long as it's very clean and the lid is not rusting or pitted. Jars and lids should be washed in hot soapy water or, better yet, run through the dishwasher.

. . . .

Pots, utensils, and bowls: The acid in vinegar reacts with certain metals such as aluminum, cast-iron (without enamel coating), and unlined copper pots. These will leach a metallic flavor into the pickles. Stainless steel, enamel- or ceramic-coated, and glass are all fine choices. The same goes for spoons, ladles, bowls, sieves, and funnels. I've been using the same wooden spoon for more than twenty years and, though it can sometimes take on flavors of previous dishes, it's not dangerous.

. . . .

Knives and slicers: A sharp knife is not only a chef's best friend, it's her safest one. More mishaps happen with dull knives because you apply more pressure when chopping. Make sure your knives are sharp and clean—you'll get better, more even, slices. I have a very old, beautiful French mandolin from my brother that has sat in a drawer unused (by me) for more than twenty years. It's big and clunky and hard to keep sharp. I much prefer less expensive plastic Japanese slicers or V-slicers for their simplicity, ease, accuracy, and perfect slices.

[METHOD] THE PROCESS OF MAKING
REFRIGERATOR PICKLES COULDN'T BE SIMPLER.

• Pack clean jars with spices and produce, then pour boiling brine (a solution of vinegar, water, salt, and sugar) into the jars. Close the lid, cool to room temperature, then refrigerate overnight.

• I steep whole spices in the brine and strained them out for several of the fruit pickles.

• For sliced cucumbers, watermelon rind, eggplant, and sliced green tomatoes, I toss them with salt and let them sit for an hour to leach out bitterness and remove some of the liquid. Then I soak them in ice water for ten minutes to re-crisp them and remove some of the salt. This really helps keep them crisp in the jar.

[STORAGE AND YIELD]

• Refrigerator pickles are kept in the fridge, where they can be safely stored for a few weeks or even as long as several months. It's pretty rare for refrigerator pickles to spoil, but it can happen. Botulism is more of a concern in processed pickles than in refrigerator pickles. Low acidity and salt, and temperatures above 50°F (10°C) breed bacterial growth, so make sure the acidity of your vinegar is at least 5 percent and your fridge is at or below 40°F (4°C). Don't be tempted to cut back on the salt or vinegar in the recipes.

• Because these are small-batch pickles that live in the fridge, the yields are usually 1 to 2 pints (475 to 950 ml) so as not to take up so much space. All of the recipes can easily be doubled, but they should be stored in the fridge, given as gifts right away, or processed for shelf stability. You can check the National Center for Home Food Preservation (http://nchfp.uga.edu/index.html) for directions.

Vegetable Pickles

Killer Diller Pickles

These dill pickles really are killer—just the right amount of garlic and dill. The recipe calls for spears, but they're equally delicious sliced and whole. If you are using whole, trim about ¼-inch (6 mm) from the ends, especially the blossom end. It contains remnants of enzymes from the blossoms that cause pickles to go mushy.

MAKES 1 QUART (950 ML)

3 large garlic cloves, sliced
1½ teaspoons coriander seeds
1½ teaspoons whole black peppercorns
1½ teaspoons yellow mustard seeds
1¼ pounds (20 ounces, or 570 g) kirby cucumbers, ends trimmed, cut into spears
8 dill sprigs
¾ cup (175 ml) white distilled vinegar
¾ cup (175 ml) water
1½ tablespoons (14 g) kosher salt

1. Place the garlic, coriander seeds, peppercorns, and mustard seeds in a clean, quart-size (950 ml) jar. Pack the cucumber spears and dill sprigs into the jar.

2. In a nonreactive saucepan, combine the vinegar, water, and salt. Bring to a boil. Pour the hot brine over the cucumbers, seal, and let cool at room temperature. Refrigerate overnight.

MAKE AHEAD

THE PICKLES WILL KEEP IN THE REFRIGERATOR FOR 4 WEEKS.

TIP: For dilly beans, a classic pickle, substitute trimmed green beans for the cucumber here.

Russian Beef Barley Soup with Pickles

MAKES 8 SERVINGS

➡ **ACTIVE: 45 MINUTES; TOTAL: 1½ HOURS**

Rassolnik, the classic Russian-Ukrainian soup made with sour pickles, is perfectly hearty and soothing in the dead of winter. The tangy pickles and pickle brine balance the richness of the meat. Use any tart pickle (*not* sweet and sour), but I especially like Killer Diller Pickles, Tangy Green Tomato Pickles, Hot-and-Sour Garlic Pickle Chips, or Pickled Asparagus.

¼ cup (59 ml) canola oil, divided
1¾ pounds (794 g) trimmed and cubed (1 inch, or 2.5 cm) chuck roast
Salt and freshly ground pepper
2 tablespoons (32 g) tomato paste
1 large onion, finely chopped (1¾ cups, or 280 g)
2 large carrots, 1 coarsely shredded (¾ cup, or 83 g), 1 sliced ¼-inch (6 mm) thick
1½ cups (135 g) finely chopped green cabbage
1½ cups (215 g) chopped pickles, preferably Killer Diller Pickles, divided
12 cups (2.8 l) low-sodium beef broth
½ cup (100 g) pearl barley
2 dried bay leaves, preferably Turkish
1 pound (455 g) potatoes, peeled and cut into ¾-inch (2 cm) pieces
2 tablespoons (6 g) chopped dill, plus more for garnish
1 cup (235 ml) strained pickle brine
Sour cream for serving

1. In a large Dutch oven, heat 2 tablespoons (30 ml) of the oil. Season the beef lightly with salt and pepper, and add half to the pot. Cook over moderately high heat until browned all over, about 10 minutes. Using a slotted spoon, transfer the beef to a plate, and brown the remaining meat. Return all of the meat to the pot and stir in the tomato paste.

2. Meanwhile, heat the remaining oil in a large skillet. Add the onion and cook over moderately high heat, stirring occasionally until softened, about 5 minutes. Add the shredded carrot and cabbage. Cook, stirring occasionally until softened and lightly browned, about 10 minutes. Add half of the chopped pickles and cook for 1 minute. Scrape the mixture into the Dutch oven. Add the broth, barley, bay leaves, and sliced carrots, and bring to a boil. Cook over low heat, partially covered, until the meat, barley, and carrots are tender, about 1 hour.

3. Add the potatoes and the remaining chopped pickles. Simmer until the potatoes are tender but not falling apart, 10 to 12 minutes longer. Stir in the dill and pickle brine, and season with salt if necessary. Serve with sour cream and chopped dill.

Spicy Bread-and-Butter Pickles

ACTIVE: 30 MINUTES; TOTAL: 1½ HOURS PLUS OVERNIGHT

Since beginning this project, I've made these pickles more often than any others—I love them that much. They're sweet and sour, spicy, crunchy, and damn delicious!

MAKES 2 PINTS (950 ML)

1½ pounds (24 ounces, or 680 g) kirby cucumbers, ends trimmed

1 small (5 ounces, or 140 g) Vidalia onion, halved lengthwise

2 tablespoons (18 g) kosher salt

¾ cup (175 ml) distilled white vinegar

¾ cup (175 ml) water

¾ cup (150 g) sugar

3 to 4 dried Asian chiles, coarsely broken

1 tablespoon (11 g) yellow mustard seeds

1 teaspoon celery seeds

½ teaspoon ground turmeric

Ice

1. Using a mandolin, slice the cucumbers ⅛-inch (3 mm) thick. Cut the onion, crosswise, ⅛-inch (3 mm) thick. Place the cucumbers and onion in a colander set in a bowl, and toss with the salt. Place a plate and heavy can on top, and refrigerate for 1 hour. Pour off the liquid, and soak the cucumbers and onion in ice water for 10 minutes. Drain and pat dry. The cucumbers should still be a bit salty.

2. In a large, nonreactive saucepan, combine the vinegar, water, sugar, chiles, mustard seeds, celery seeds, and turmeric. Bring to a boil. Off the heat, add the cucumbers and onion. Spoon and ladle the mixture into 2 clean, pint-size (475 ml) jars. Seal and let cool at room temperature. Refrigerate overnight.

MAKE AHEAD

THE PICKLES WILL KEEP IN THE REFRIGERATOR FOR 4 WEEKS.

Pickle-Brined Chicken

Debating whether to do grilled or fried chicken here, my waistline won the battle. But this brining method is amazing with fried chicken. Find your favorite recipe, skipping their brine in favor of this pickle brine, and knock yourself out! (You may want to run a few more miles, though.)

MAKES 4 TARTINES

 ACTIVE: 30 MINUTES; TOTAL: 30 MINUTES PLUS 4 HOURS

1¼ cups (295 ml) unstrained brine from Killer Diller Pickles, Spicy Bread-and-Butter Pickles, Tangy Green Tomato Pickles, or Hot-and-Sour Garlic Pickle Chips (pg 17, 21, 88, or 30)
¼ cup (60 ml) water
2 boneless, skinless chicken breasts, butterflied
6 boneless, skinless chicken thighs
Extra-virgin olive oil
Salt and freshly ground pepper

1. In a sealable plastic bag, combine the brine, water, chicken breasts, and chicken thighs. Press out the air, seal the bag, and refrigerate for 4 to 6 hours.

2. Light a grill and oil the grates. Drain the chicken, picking off the solids, and pat dry. Brush the chicken with oil, and season lightly with salt and pepper. Grill over high heat, turning once, until lightly charred and cooked through, about 12 minutes. Serve with pickles!

Curried Pickle Spears

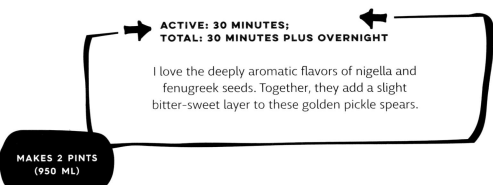

**ACTIVE: 30 MINUTES;
TOTAL: 30 MINUTES PLUS OVERNIGHT**

I love the deeply aromatic flavors of nigella and fenugreek seeds. Together, they add a slight bitter-sweet layer to these golden pickle spears.

**MAKES 2 PINTS
(950 ML)**

2 large garlic cloves, thinly sliced
1 tablespoon (8 g) julienned fresh
  ginger
1 teaspoon nigella seeds
1 teaspoon fenugreek seeds
1 teaspoon brown or yellow
  mustard seeds
1¼ pounds (20 ounces, or 570 g)
  kirby cucumbers, ends trimmed,
  cut into spears
¾ cup (175 ml) distilled white
  vinegar
¾ cup (175 ml) water
1½ tablespoons (14 g) kosher salt
1½ teaspoons Madras curry powder
½ teaspoon turmeric

1. Divide the garlic, ginger, nigella seeds, fenugreek seeds, and mustard seeds between 2 clean, pint-size (475 ml) jars. Pack the cucumber spears into the jars.

2. In a nonreactive saucepan, combine the vinegar, water, salt, curry powder, and turmeric. Bring to a boil. Pour the hot brine over the cucumbers, seal, and let cool at room temperature. Refrigerate overnight.

**MAKE
AHEAD**

THE PICKLES WILL KEEP IN THE REFRIGERATOR FOR 4 WEEKS.

Pickled Egg Tartine

MAKES 4 EGGS

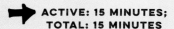

ACTIVE: 15 MINUTES;
TOTAL: 15 MINUTES

¼ cup plus 2 tablespoons
   (84 g) mayonnaise
1 oil-packed anchovy fillet,
   mashed
Freshly ground black pepper
4 slices multigrain bread,
   toasted
1 small Hass avocado, thinly
   sliced
4 pickled eggs, sliced
2 tablespoons (6 g) minced
   chives

Such an easy and delicious go-to sandwich, the tartine is France's answer to the bruschetta. All it is is an open-faced sandwich. This combo—eggs, avocado, and anchovy—is made exponentially more interesting with the addition of pickled eggs.

In a small bowl, combine the mayonnaise and anchovy, and season with pepper. Spread the mixture on the toast, and top with avocado, eggs, and chives. Cut each tartine in half and serve.

Inside-Out Pickled Eggs

ACTIVE: 15 MINUTES; TOTAL:
15 MINUTES, PLUS 2 DAYS

MAKES 4 EGGS

4 large eggs
Pickle brine from 1 pint (475 g) Curried Pickle Spears

Put the eggs into a medium saucepan, cover with cold water, and bring to a vigorous boil. Cover and let sit off the heat for 10 minutes. Drain and crack the eggs by gently shaking the pan. Fill with cold water and let cool slightly. Peel and transfer the eggs to a sealable plastic bag. Add the brine and seal the bag, pressing out the air. Refrigerate for 2 days, turning the bag occasionally, until the eggs are bright yellow.

MAKE AHEAD THE EGGS CAN SIT IN THE BRINE FOR UP TO 4 DAYS.

Fried Pickles with Ranch

 ACTIVE: 30 MINUTES; TOTAL: 30 MINUTES

I remember the first time I had really good fried pickles was at an upscale burger joint in Manhattan. They were crispy, tangy, and delicious, and they cost some *ridiculous* amount of money. Down south, they're just as good, more plentiful, and a fraction of the cost. They are, after all, fried pickles! You can keep them warm in a hot oven, but they're never as good as they are fresh out of the pan.

MAKES 3 TO 4 SERVINGS

1 cup (125 g) all-purpose flour
¼ cup (35 g) fine-ground cornmeal
1½ tablespoons (11 g) Old Bay Seasoning
½ teaspoon cayenne pepper
1 pint (475 ml) pickle chips, preferably Hot-and-Sour Garlic Pickle Chips, drained and patted dry, plus 1 tablespoon (15 ml) pickle brine, divided
1 cup (235 ml) buttermilk, divided
½ cup (115 g) mayonnaise
Salt and freshly ground pepper
1 large egg
Oil for frying

1. In a sealable plastic bag, combine the flour, cornmeal, Old Bay, and cayenne. Add the pickle chips, seal the bag, and shake to coat. Transfer the pickles to a plate, leaving the dry ingredients in the bag.

2. In a small bowl, make the dipping sauce by whisking ½ cup (120 ml) of the buttermilk with the mayonnaise and pickle brine. Season with salt and pepper. Set aside.

3. In a shallow bowl of pie plate, beat the egg with the remaining buttermilk.

4. Heat 1 inch (2.5 cm) of oil in a large cast-iron skillet until shimmering. Working in large batches, dip the pickles in the egg mixture, then dredge in the reserved flour mixture. Fry over moderate heat, turning once, until golden and crisp, about 3 minutes. Drain on paper towels and sprinkle lightly with salt. Serve right away with the ranch dipping sauce, while you fry the remaining pickles.

Hot-and-Sour Garlic Pickle Chips

**MAKES 2 PINTS
(950 ML)**

The longer these pickles sit, the spicier they become. These are also great as spears or whole. In that case, you can skip the salting in step 1 and just add the salt to the brine.

**ACTIVE: 30 MINUTES;
TOTAL: 1½ HOURS
PLUS OVERNIGHT**

1½ pounds (24 ounces, or 680 g)
  kirby cucumbers, ends trimmed
2 tablespoons (18 g) kosher salt
1½ tablespoons (8 g) coriander
  seeds
1½ teaspoons yellow mustard seeds
4 dried Asian chiles, coarsely
  broken
2 bay leaves, preferably Turkish
4 garlic cloves, thinly sliced
1 cup (235 ml) distilled white
  vinegar
¾ cup (175 ml) water

1. Using a mandolin, slice the cucumbers ⅛-inch (3 mm) thick. Place the cucumbers in a colander set in a bowl, and toss with the salt. Place a plate and heavy can on top, and refrigerate for 1 hour. Pour off the liquid and soak the cucumbers in ice water for 10 minutes. Drain and pat dry. The cucumbers should still be a bit salty. Wipe out the bowl.

2. Return the cucumbers to the bowl along with the coriander seeds, mustard seeds, chiles, bay leaves, and garlic. Toss to combine. Pack 2 clean, pint-size (475 ml) jars with the mixture.

3. In a small nonreactive saucepan, combine the vinegar and water. Bring to a boil. Pour the hot brine into the jars, seal, and let cool at room temperature. Refrigerate overnight.

**MAKE
AHEAD**

THE PICKLES WILL
KEEP IN THE
REFRIGERATOR FOR
4 WEEKS.

Pickled Plum Tomatoes with Chipotle

MAKES 1 QUART (950 ML)

One of my favorite things to do with end-of-season, bumper crop tomatoes is make tomato marmelata, a sweet/spicy tomato jam. It's pretty involved—peeling, seeding, and chopping the tomatoes, then cooking them long and slowly with sugar, vinegar, and spices. These pickles are a less labor-intensive nod, and equally delicious. Great stirred into warm pasta, on sandwiches, hot dogs, burgers, and so on.

 ACTIVE: 30 MIN; TOTAL: 30 MIN PLUS OVERNIGHT

1½ pounds (680 g) firm but ripe plum tomatoes, cored
1 cinnamon stick (4-inches, or 10.2 cm)
2 small dried chipotles (or 2 teaspoons chipotle flakes)
½ cup (120 ml) distilled white vinegar
¼ cup (60 ml) water
½ cup (100 g) sugar
1 teaspoon Kosher salt

1. Bring a large saucepan of water to a boil. Make a shallow X in the bottoms of each tomato. Fill a bowl with ice water. Blanch the tomatoes in the boiling water for 30 seconds, just until the skins begin to loosen. Using a slotted spoon, transfer the tomatoes to the ice water and let cool. Peel the tomatoes and cut into quarters, lengthwise. Pat dry.

2. Pack the tomatoes, cinnamon stick, and chipotles into a clean, quart-size (950 ml) jar.

3. In a small, nonreactive saucepan, combine the vinegar, water, sugar, and salt and bring to a boil. Pour the hot brine into the jar, seal and and let cool at room temperature. Refrigerate overnight.

MAKE AHEAD

THE PICKLES WILL KEEP IN THE REFRIGERATOR FOR 4 WEEKS.

Pickled Radish Chips

When radishes hit vinegar, watch out. They're awful stinky! (But oh so delicious, especially hot spicy radishes.) That's why I only make them in small batches. Because they're sliced so thinly, you can use them as soon as they cool, which you can speed up by pickling them in a shallow bowl. Cover it, of course, with plastic and chill it in the fridge.

MAKES ½ PINT (235 ML)

ACTIVE: 15 MINUTES; TOTAL: 15 MINUTES PLUS COOLING

4 large red radishes, very thinly sliced
½ teaspoon nigella seeds
½ teaspoon pink peppercorns, crushed
¼ cup (60 ml) rice vinegar
2 tablespoons (28 ml) water
1 tablespoon (13 g) sugar
1 teaspoon kosher salt

Put the radishes, nigella seeds, and peppercorns into a clean, ½-pint (235 ml) jar. In a small saucepan, combine the vinegar, water, sugar, and salt. Bring to a boil. Pour the hot brine into the jar, seal, and let cool at room temperature. Refrigerate overnight.

MAKE AHEAD THE PICKLES WILL KEEP IN THE REFRIGERATOR FOR 1 WEEK.

Pickled Sweet Beets with Pearl Onions

ACTIVE: 45 MINUTES;
TOTAL: 1½ HOURS PLUS OVERNIGHT

As a kid, I hated beets—they were always too sweet and bland. But *pickled* beets were a real game changer. The acid balances the sweetness and the caraway adds a nice undertone. They're great in salads, layered with cream cheese and lox on a bagel, or puréed into an instant borscht shooter. Plus the cute pink onions are great in martinis.

MAKES 2 PINTS (950 ML)

1¼ cups (156 g) red or white pearl onions, ends trimmed

4 medium beets (about 1½ pounds, or 680 g), trimmed

2 bay leaves, preferably Turkish

1 teaspoon coriander seeds

½ teaspoon caraway seeds

¾ cup (175 ml) distilled white vinegar

¾ cup (175 ml) water

¾ cup (150 g) sugar

1 tablespoon (9 g) kosher salt

1. Bring a large pot of water to a boil. Add the onions and blanch until barely tender, about 3 minutes. Using a slotted spoon, transfer the onions to a bowl and let cool slightly. Slip the skins off the onions. *See note.*

2. Return the water to a boil and add the beets. Cook until tender, about 45 minutes. Drain and let cool slightly. Peel the beets. Halve lengthwise and then cut until into ½-inch (1 cm)-thick slices. Divide the onions, beets, bay leaves, coriander seeds, and caraway seeds between 2 clean, pint-size (475 ml) jars.

3. In a small, nonreactive saucepan, combine the vinegar, water, sugar, and salt. Bring to a boil. Pour the hot brine into the jars, seal, and let cool at room temperature. Refrigerate overnight.

Note: Alternatively, you can use frozen pearl onions; just omit the boiling.

MAKE AHEAD

THE PICKLES WILL KEEP IN THE REFRIGERATOR FOR 2 WEEKS.

Super Quick Borscht

At your next cocktail party serve these in twelve shot glasses for chilled borscht shooters.

MAKES 4 FIRST-COURSE SERVINGS

 ACTIVE: 15 MINUTES; TOTAL: 15 MINUTES

1 cup (227 g) Pickled Sweet Beets with Pearl Onions, plus ¾ cup (175 ml) brine
½ cup (120 ml) chicken broth
2 teaspoons horseradish, plus more for garnish
Sour cream and chopped dill for serving

In a blender, combine the beets and onions, brine, broth, and horseradish. Purée until smooth. Transfer to a saucepan and bring to a boil. Simmer, partially covered, for 10 minutes. Return the soup to the blender for a silky texture. Serve hot or chilled, garnished with sour cream, dill, and horseradish.

Sunchoke Pickle Relish

MAKES 2 PINTS (950 ML)

➤ **ACTIVE: 1 HOUR; TOTAL: 2 HOURS PLUS OVERNIGHT**

1 lemon, halved
1¼ pounds (570 g) large sunchokes
1 yellow pepper, cored and cut into ½-inch (1 cm) dice
¼ cup (40 g) coarsely chopped Vidalia onion
¼ cup (38 g) kosher salt
4 dried Asian chiles
1 tablespoon (11 g) yellow mustard seeds
1 teaspoon celery seeds
¾ cup (175 ml) cider vinegar
¾ cup (175 ml) water
¾ cup (150 g) sugar
1 teaspoon ground turmeric

Very similar to Bread-and-Butter Pickles, the brine is sweet and sour, yellow from turmeric, and incredibly addictive. The exception is that sunchokes are nutty and super crunchy.

1. Squeeze the lemon into a large bowl of water, discarding any seeds. Peel the sunchokes, adding them to the water to prevent oxidizing. Using a sturdy knife, cut the sunchokes into ¼ x 1-inch (6 mm x 2.5 cm) matchsticks, returning them to the water to prevent oxidizing. Add the yellow pepper, onion, and salt to the water. Refrigerate for 1 hour. Drain the vegetables, shaking off the excess water, but don't rinse. The vegetables should be a bit salty. Divide the mixture between 2 clean, pint-size (475 ml) jars. Divide the chiles, mustard seeds, and celery seeds between the jars.

2. In a small, nonreactive saucepan, combine the vinegar, water, sugar, and turmeric. Bring to a boil. Pour the hot brine into the jars, seal, and let cool at room temperature. Refrigerate overnight.

MAKE AHEAD

THE PICKLES WILL KEEP IN THE REFRIGERATOR FOR 4 WEEKS.

USES FOR SUNCHOKE PICKLES:

- Add the pickles and brine to coleslaw
- Substitute the brine for mustard, sugar, and vinegar in baked beans
- Use as a hot dog topper

Pickled Ginger

Sure you can buy pickled ginger at most supermarkets now, but it's not nearly as delicious as homemade. It's really worth a try—especially because fresh, beautiful produce is more widely available than ever before. Look for plump ginger with tight skin and no wrinkles. The easiest way to peel ginger is to scrape it with a small teaspoon.

MAKES ½ PINT (235 ML)

 ACTIVE: 15 MINUTES; TOTAL: 15 MINUTES PLUS OVERNIGHT

4 ounces (115 g) fresh young ginger, peeled and very thinly sliced (1 cup)
2 teaspoons salt, divided
½ cup (120 ml) rice vinegar
¼ cup (50 g) sugar

1. Bring a small saucepan of water to a boil. Add the ginger and blanch for 30 seconds. Drain and cool. Sprinkle the ginger with ½ teaspoon of the salt and transfer to a clean, ½-pint (235 ml) jar.

2. In the same saucepan, combine the vinegar, sugar, and remaining 1½ teaspoons salt. Bring to a boil. Pour the hot brine into the jar, seal, and let cool at room temperature. Refrigerate overnight.

MAKE AHEAD

THE PICKLES WILL KEEP IN THE REFRIGERATOR FOR 4 WEEKS.

Yellow Wax Beans with Garlic and Tarragon

ACTIVE: 20 MINUTES; TOTAL: 20 MINUTES PLUS OVERNIGHT

Equally delicious with any type of bean, these pickles makes a great addition to niçoise, three-bean salad, grain salads, stir-fries, grilled veggie subs, or wrapped in prosciutto and grilled.

MAKES 1 PINT (475 ML)

1 garlic clove, sliced
1 bay leaf, preferably Turkish
½ teaspoon white peppercorns
½ teaspoon coriander seeds
½ teaspoon mustard seeds
8 ounces (225 g) yellow wax beans, trimmed to fit
4 sprigs (2 inches, or 5 cm, each) tarragon
½ cup (120 ml) white wine vinegar
½ cup (120 ml) water
2 teaspoons kosher salt

1. Put the garlic, bay leaf, peppercorns, coriander seeds, and mustard seeds into a clean, pint-size (475 ml) jar. Pack the beans and tarragon into the jar.

2. In a small, nonreactive saucepan, combine the vinegar, water, and salt. Bring to a boil. Pour the hot brine into the jar, seal, and let cool at room temperature. Refrigerate overnight.

MAKE AHEAD

THE PICKLES WILL KEEP IN THE REFRIGERATOR FOR 2 WEEKS.

Pickled Asparagus with Dill and Coriander

MAKES 2 PINTS (950 ML)

➡ **ACTIVE: 30 MINUTES; TOTAL: 30 MINUTES PLUS OVERNIGHT**

1 bay leaf, preferably Turkish
1 teaspoon coriander seeds
1 teaspoon whole black peppercorns
1 pound (455 g) medium-thick asparagus
4 small dill sprigs
1 medium shallot, thinly sliced into rings
1¼ cups (295 ml) white wine vinegar
1¼ cups (295 ml) water
1 tablespoon (9 g) kosher salt

These pickles are a cool riff on dilly beans. I love serving these dramatic asparagus spears at cocktail parties as part of a crudité platter with a creamy dip.

1. Place the bay leaf, coriander seeds, and peppercorns into clean, tall, narrow jar (or 2 pint-size [475 ml] jars). Trim the asparagus to fit and peel the ends if thicker than ½ inch (1 cm). Pack the asparagus, dill, and shallots into the jar (or jars).

2. In a small, nonreactive saucepan, combine the vinegar, water, and salt. Bring to a boil. Pour the hot brine into the jar, seal, and let cool at room temperature. Refrigerate overnight.

MAKE AHEAD

THE PICKLES WILL KEEP IN THE REFRIGERATOR FOR 2 WEEKS.

Smoky Okra Pickles

 ACTIVE: 20 MINUTES; TOTAL: 20 MINUTES PLUS OVERNIGHT

Okra is one of those vegetables that took some time to grow on me. I think fried okra may've actually broken through and made way for all the other wonderful applications. Pickled okra stay pretty crunchy in the jar, but can get a little slimy on the outside. Just shake 'em off before putting them on your plate.

MAKES 1 PINT (475 ML)

6 ounces (170 g) okra pods (about 4 inches, or 10 cm, long)
3 dried Asian chiles
1 garlic clove, thinly sliced
¾ cup (175 ml) distilled white vinegar
¾ cup (175 ml) water
1½ teaspoons smoked salt
1½ teaspoons smoked hot paprika

1. Trim the stem ends to ½ inch (1 cm) and pack the okra, chiles, and garlic into a clean, pint-size (475 ml) jar.

2. In a small, nonreactive saucepan, combine the vinegar, water, smoked salt, and smoked paprika. Bring to a boil. Pour the hot brine into the jar, seal, and let cool at room temperature. Refrigerate overnight.

MAKE AHEAD

THE PICKLES WILL KEEP IN THE REFRIGERATOR FOR 2 WEEKS.

Ginger-Pickled Snap Peas

These tart, spicy pickles stay crisp for a pretty long time, making them perfect for stir-fries, crudité, and salads.

MAKES 1 PINT (475 ML)

 ACTIVE: 20 MINUTES; TOTAL: 20 MINUTES PLUS OVERNIGHT

2 tablespoons (16 g) finely julienned fresh ginger

2 dried Asian chiles

1 garlic clove, sliced

6 ounces (175 g) snap peas, stemmed and stringed

½ cup (120 ml) distilled white vinegar

½ cup (120 ml) water

1 tablespoon (9 g) kosher salt

1 tablespoon (13 g) sugar

1. Put the ginger, chiles, and garlic into a clean, pint-size (475 ml) jar. Pack the snap peas into the jar.

2. In a small, nonreactive saucepan, combine the vinegar, water, salt, and sugar. Bring to a boil. Pour the hot brine into the jar, seal, and let cool at room temperature. Refrigerate overnight.

MAKE AHEAD

THE PICKLES WILL KEEP IN THE REFRIGERATOR FOR 2 WEEKS.

Stir-Fried Shrimp with Ginger-Pickled Snap Peas

4 SERVINGS

ACTIVE: 20 MINUTES; TOTAL: 20 MINUTES

½ cup (120 ml) chicken stock

2 tablespoons (28 ml) soy sauce

1 cup (160 g) Ginger-Pickled Snap Peas, sliced, plus 1 tablespoon (15 ml) each of the ginger and pickle brine, divided

1 teaspoon Chinese chile garlic sauce

1 tablespoon (13 g) sugar

1 teaspoon cornstarch

2 tablespoons (28 ml) vegetable oil

1 garlic clove, minced

1 pound (455 g) peeled and deveined medium shrimp

2 scallions, white and green, thinly sliced on the diagonal

This simple stir-fry uses Ginger-Pickled Snap Peas, the ginger, and a bit of the brine to give the sauce some tang. Serve it with rice or noodles.

1. In a small bowl, whisk the chicken stock, soy sauce, pickle brine, chile garlic sauce, sugar, and cornstarch.

2. Heat the oil in a wok or nonstick skillet until small puffs of smoke appear. Add the ginger and garlic, and stir-fry over moderately high heat until softened and just beginning to brown, 2 minutes. Add the snap peas and stir-fry for 1 minute. Add the shrimp and stir-fry until nearly cooked through, 1 minute. Add the scallions and stir-fry just until wilted, 30 seconds. Whisk the liquid, add it to the pan, and stir-fry until the shrimp are cooked through and the sauce is thickened, about 1 minute longer.

Pickled Shallots with Rosemary and Lemon

**MAKES 1 PINT
(475 ML)**

➡️ **ACTIVE: 20 MINUTES;
TOTAL: 20 MINUTES PLUS
OVERNIGHT**

5 medium shallots, peeled and cut
   into thin wedges
1 sprig (4-inches, or 10 cm)
   rosemary, broken
6 strips (2 inches, or 5 cm, each)
   lemon zest removed with
   vegetable peeler
1 teaspoon whole black
   peppercorns
½ cup (120 ml) white wine vinegar
   (or distilled white vinegar)
¾ cup (175 ml) water
3 tablespoons (39 g) sugar
1½ tablespoons (14 g) kosher salt

Heady with rosemary and lemon, these pickled shallots
(aside from just eating them out of the jar) make an
awesome addition to vinaigrettes, aioli, pesto, meatballs,
or anywhere else you'd add chopped shallots.

1. Pack the shallots, rosemary, lemon
zest, and peppercorns into a clean,
pint-size (475 ml) jar.

2. In a small, nonreactive saucepan,
combine the vinegar, water, sugar, and
salt. Bring to a boil. Pour the hot brine
into the jar, seal, and let cool at room
temperature. Refrigerate overnight.

**MAKE
AHEAD**

THE PICKLES WILL
KEEP IN THE
REFRIGERATOR FOR
4 WEEKS.

Pickled Shallot Mignonette

Sweet, briny oysters are enlivened by the sweet-tart shallots in this super simple mignonette sauce.

TOTAL: 5 MINUTES

1 tablespoon (10 g) minced Pickled Shallots with Rosemary and Lemon, plus ¼ cup (60 ml) strained brine

1 teaspoon coarsely ground black pepper

12 oysters on the half shell, freshly shucked

In a small bowl, combine the minced shallots, brine, and pepper, and chill. Spoon over oysters and serve.

Pickled Ramps

The window for these precious wild leeks is open for such a short time. Get them while they're available and pickle the bulbs. The green leafy tops make a super delicious pesto, but I also like thinly slicing them and stirring them into hot buttery noodles.

**MAKES 1 PINT
(475 ML)**

➤ **ACTIVE: 30 MINUTES;
TOTAL: 30 MINUTES
PLUS OVERNIGHT**

12 ounces (340 g) ramps,
    washed well
1 teaspoon coriander seeds
1 teaspoon whole white
    peppercorns
1 bay leaf, preferably Turkish
½ star anise
½ cup (120 ml) distilled white
    vinegar
⅔ cup (160 ml) water
⅓ cup (67 g) sugar
1 tablespoon (9 g) kosher salt

1. Trim the green leafy tops of the ramps about 1 inch (2.5 cm) from where the white/red parts end. Pack the ramp bulbs into a clean, pint-size (475 ml) jar, and add the coriander seeds, peppercorns, bay leaf, and star anise.

2. In a small, nonreactive saucepan, combine the vinegar, water, sugar, and salt. Bring to a boil. Pour the hot brine into the jar, seal, and let cool at room temperature. Refrigerate overnight.

**MAKE
AHEAD**

THE PICKLES WILL
KEEP IN THE
REFRIGERATOR FOR
4 WEEKS.

Pickled Leeks and Asparagus

MAKES 1 PINT (475 ML)

When buying leeks for this recipe, look for ones that are no more than an inch (2.5 cm) wide. The younger leeks are, the more tender and sweet they are; important here because they are not cooked. If thin leeks aren't available, large scallions will be just fine.

ACTIVE: 20 MINUTES; TOTAL: 20 MINUTES PLUS OVERNIGHT

½ teaspoon yellow mustard seeds
½ teaspoon whole black peppercorns
2 small leeks, halved lengthwise, washed well
4 ounces (115 g) medium-thin asparagus
4 sprigs (2 inches, or 5 cm, each) tarragon
½ cup (120 ml) white wine vinegar
½ cup (120 ml) water
2 teaspoons salt

1. Put the mustard seeds and peppercorns into a clean, pint-size (475 ml) jar. Keeping the leeks intact, trim them to fit the jar. Trim the asparagus to fit the jar. Pack the leeks, asparagus, and tarragon into the jar.

2. In a small, nonreactive saucepan, combine the vinegar, water, and salt. Bring to a boil. Pour the hot brine into the jar, seal, and let cool at room temperature. Refrigerate overnight.

Pickled Asparagus Remoulade

What's not to love about a remoulade sauce? Especially when it's paired with crab cakes, fried fish, hush puppies, or maybe even fried pickles?

MAKES ABOUT 1 CUP (250 G)

 ACTIVE: 10 MINUTES; TOTAL: 10 MINUTES

1 cup (225 g) mayonnaise
1 tablespoon (16 g) Dijon mustard
3 tablespoons (about 30 g) chopped Pickled Leeks and Asparagus, plus 1 tablespoon (15 ml) pickle brine
1 tablespoon (4 g) chopped tarragon
1 garlic clove, mashed to a paste
Salt and freshly ground pepper

In a bowl, combine the mayonnaise, mustard, leeks and asparagus, pickle brine, tarragon, and garlic. Season with salt and pepper.

Italian-Style Pickled Eggplant

MAKES 1 QUART (950 ML)

➡ **ACTIVE: 30 MINUTES; TOTAL: 30 MINUTES PLUS OVERNIGHT**

¾ cup (175 ml) extra-virgin olive oil
3 garlic cloves, thinly sliced
1 teaspoon fennel seeds
½ teaspoon crushed red pepper flakes
1½ pounds (680 g) eggplant, cut into ½ x 1-inch (1 x 2.5 cm) strips
1 cup (235 ml) white distilled vinegar
½ cup (120 ml) water
1 tablespoon (9 g) kosher salt
1 tablespoon (13 g) sugar
2 tablespoons (5 g) thinly sliced basil

I watched my grandmother make jars and jars of pickled eggplant every summer from the eggplant growing in our garden. Hers was just straight up vinegar and salt. My dad loved it, but I never much cared for it—too tart. It wasn't until I was older that I came to appreciate it. Mine is balanced with garlic, spices, herbs, and a healthy dose of extra-virgin olive oil. Try this on big crusty, cheesy sandwiches, or tossed with warm pasta, or with grilled lamb or pork.

1. Heat the oil in a large, nonstick skillet. Add the garlic and cook over moderately high heat, stirring, until fragrant, about 1 minute. Add the fennel and crushed red pepper, and cook until fragrant, about 20 seconds. Add the eggplant and cook, stirring occasionally, until tender and browned in spots, 8 to 10 minutes.

2. Add the vinegar, water, salt, and sugar. Bring to a boil. Simmer over moderate heat until the liquid is slightly reduced, about 5 minutes. Stir in the basil and spoon into a clean, quart-size (950 ml) jar. Let cool at room temperature and refrigerate overnight.

MAKE AHEAD

THE PICKLES WILL KEEP IN THE REFRIGERATOR FOR 4 WEEKS.

Pickled Thai Eggplant

ACTIVE: 30 MINUTES; TOTAL: 30 MINUTES PLUS 2 DAYS

Thai eggplants differ from other eggplant varieties in their size, shape, and color. Thai eggplants are small, round, and green with white stripes. Their size makes them ideal for pickling whole, just be sure to poke them all over with a skewer to allow the brine to seep in. Once pickled, they're great in stir-fries, thinly sliced in sandwiches, added to curries, and even cut in half and grilled.

MAKES 1 QUART (950 ML)

2 garlic cloves, sliced

1 lemongrass stalk, bottom 6 inches (15 cm) thinly sliced

1 tablespoon (15 g) Thai ground chiles in soybean oil (alternatively sambal oelek or Chinese chile garlic sauce)

1 pound (455 g) Thai eggplant, stemmed

1 cup (235 ml) distilled white vinegar

1 cup (235 ml) water

3 tablespoons (27 g) kosher salt

1 tablespoon (18 g) Asian fish sauce

1. Put the garlic, lemongrass, and ground chiles into a clean, quart-size (950 ml) jar. Using a sharp knife, trim a thin sliver from the stem end of each eggplant. Using a skewer or toothpick, prick the eggplant all over, and pack them into the jar.

2. In a medium, nonreactive saucepan, combine the vinegar, water, salt, and fish sauce. Bring to a boil. Pour the hot brine into the jar, seal, and let cool at room temperature. Refrigerate overnight.

MAKE AHEAD

THE PICKLES WILL KEEP IN THE REFRIGERATOR FOR 2 MONTHS.

Turkey Larb with Pickled Thai Eggplant

ACTIVE: 30 MINUTES; TOTAL: 45 MINUTES

Larb, a popular dish from Laos and parts of southeast Asia, is a minced meat and vegetable salad. It's tossed with a tangy dressing of lime juice, fish sauce, and sugar, and it's served in lettuce leaves. I've added pickled eggplant to the meat mixture and the tangy, spicy pickle brine to the dressing.

MAKES 4 TO 5 SERVINGS

DRESSING
1 tablespoon (18 g) Thai or Vietnamese fish sauce
1 tablespoon (15 ml) lime juice
2 tablespoons (26 g) sugar
3 tablespoons (45 ml) brine from Pickled Thai Eggplant

LARB
1 pound (455 g) ground turkey
1 large shallot, thinly sliced
2 keffir lime leaves, very thinly sliced
1 to 2 Thai chiles, thinly sliced
1 cup (136 g) diced Pickled Thai Eggplant
1½ tablespoons (15 g) strained garlic/lemongrass from the brine
1 tablespoon (18 g) Thai or Vietnamese fish sauce
Kosher salt
3 tablespoons (45 ml) canola or peanut oil
2 tablespoons (12 g) chopped mint
2 tablespoons (2 g) chopped cilantro
2 tablespoons (5 g) chopped Thai basil
Lettuce leaves, steamed rice, chopped peanuts, and lime wedges for serving

1. FOR THE DRESSING: In a small bowl, whisk all of the dressing ingredients until the sugar dissolves.

2. FOR THE LARB: In a large bowl, combine the turkey, shallots, lime leaves, chiles, eggplant, garlic/lemongrass mixture, and fish sauce. Season with a pinch of salt.

3. In a large, sturdy nonstick skillet, heat the oil. Add the turkey mixture and cook, breaking up the lumps with a wooden spoon until all of the liquid is evaporated and the mixture is golden brown in spots, about 14 minutes. Off the heat, stir in the herbs and dressing, and transfer to a bowl. Serve the larb in lettuce leaves with rice, peanuts, and a squirt of lime.

Sweet Ginger Watermelon Rind

➤ **ACTIVE: 30 MINUTES; TOTAL: 1½ HOURS PLUS OVERNIGHT**

Having spent quite a bit of time in the south, I was introduced to pickled watermelon rinds, a popular player at most picnics and potlucks. I remember thinking it was odd to use something my mother insisted would give me a bellyache, but here they are— crunchy, sweet, and tangy. And the only reason you *might* get a bellyache is that they're so deliciously addictive, it's hard to stop eating them.

MAKES 2 PINTS (950 ML)

¼ large watermelon

2 tablespoons (18 g) kosher salt

4 strips (2 inches, or 5 cm, each) lime zest, finely julienned

1 piece (1 x 2 inches, or 2.5 x 5 cm) fresh ginger, peeled and finely julienned (about 2 tablespoons, or 16 g)

¾ cup (175 ml) distilled white vinegar

¾ cup (175 ml) water

¾ cup (150 g) sugar

1. Cut the watermelon into 1-inch (2.5 cm) slices. Remove the flesh, leaving about ¼ inch (6 mm) attached to the rind, and reserve it for another use. Peel the rind with a vegetable peeler. Cut the rind into ½ x 1-inch (1 x 2.5 cm) pieces, and transfer them to a colander set in a bowl. Toss the rind with the salt, and refrigerate for 1 hour.

2. Pour off the liquid. Soak the watermelon rind in ice water with the lime zest and ginger for 10 minutes. Drain, shaking off the excess water. Transfer to 2 clean, pint-size (475 ml) jars.

3. In a large, nonreactive saucepan, combine the vinegar, water, and sugar. Bring to a boil. Pour the hot brine into the jars, seal, and let cool at room temperature. Refrigerate overnight.

MAKE AHEAD

THE PICKLES WILL KEEP IN THE REFRIGERATOR FOR 4 WEEKS.

➤ **TIP:** Stir a few tablespoons (45 ml) of the brine into hot, short-grain rice for instant sushi rice.

Zucchini Piccalilli

MAKES 1 QUART (950 ML) AND ½ PINT (235 ML)

1½ pounds (680 g) small zucchini, cut into ½-inch (1 cm) cubes

1 small Vidalia onion, cut into ½-inch (1 cm) cubes

2 tablespoons (18 g) kosher salt

1 tablespoon (11 g) yellow mustard seeds

1½ teaspoons dried mustard powder

1½ teaspoons ground turmeric

1 teaspoon celery seeds

1 teaspoon fenugreek seeds

1 tablespoon (8 g) cornstarch

1 cup (200 g) sugar

2 cups (475 ml) distilled white vinegar

1 red bell pepper, cut into ½-inch (1 cm) cubes

1 serrano chile, thinly sliced (seeded optional)

Tired of zucchini bread? Don't want to fry zucchini fritters? Looking for yet another way to use up all the zucchini from your garden? This piccalilli is the perfect answer. You can easily double the recipe and give it to friends.

1. Place the zucchini and onion in a colander set in a bowl, and toss with the salt. Place a plate and heavy can on top, and refrigerate for 1 hour. Pour off the liquid, and soak the zucchini and onion in ice water for 10 minutes. Drain and pat dry. The zucchini should still be a bit salty.

2. In a large, nonreactive saucepan, combine the mustard seeds, dried mustard, turmeric, celery seeds, fenugreek seeds, cornstarch, and sugar. Whisk in ½ cup (120 ml) of the vinegar to form a smooth paste, then whisk in the remaining vinegar. Bring to a boil, whisking, until bubbling and slightly thickened, about 5 minutes. Add the zucchini, onion, bell pepper, and serrano chile. Return just to the boil. Off the heat, spoon and ladle the mixture into 1 clean, quart-size (950 ml) jar and 1 clean, ½-pint (235 ml) jar. Seal and let cool at room temperature. Refrigerate overnight.

MAKE AHEAD

THE PICCALILLI WILL KEEP IN THE REFRIGERATOR FOR 4 WEEKS.

Almost-Instant Kimchi

 ACTIVE: 30 MINUTES; TOTAL: 30 MINUTES PLUS OVERNIGHT

I was so worried that my fridge would stink if I left the jar in there for more than two weeks, but this kimchi is so delicious and so versatile, it didn't last the *weekend*. It's amazing chopped and added to rice, stir-fries, hot dogs, grilled cheese, and lots more. One of my favorites is to cook it on a hot griddle until lightly caramelized, and serve it with sliced skirt steak in a corn tortilla.

MAKES 1 QUART (950 ML)

- 1 small Napa cabbage, about 1½ pounds (680 g)
- 4 tablespoons (36 g) kosher salt
- ¼ cup (50 g) sugar, divided
- 4 tablespoons (40 g) minced garlic (8 large cloves)
- 2 tablespoons (12 g) minced peeled ginger
- ¼ cup (60 g) kochugaru (Korean pepper flakes)
- ¼ cup (72 g) Asian fish sauce
- 2 tablespoons (28 ml) light soy sauce
- 1 tablespoon (15 ml) rice vinegar
- 3 large scallions, halved lengthwise and cut into 1-inch (2.5 cm) lengths
- 1 large carrot, coarsely shredded
- 2 tablespoons (16 g) toasted sesame seed

1. Trim the root end from the Napa cabbage and separate the leaves. Stacking the leaves, cut them in half lengthwise. Place the cabbage in a bowl along with the salt and 1 tablespoon (13 g) of the sugar and gently massage until slightly wilted. Refrigerate for 1 hour until wilted. Drain and rinse the cabbage. Squeeze out excess water and pat dry.

2. In a large bowl, combine the remaining 3 tablespoons (37 g) sugar with the garlic, ginger, kochugaru, fish sauce, soy sauce, and vinegar. Add the cabbage, scallions, carrot, and sesame seeds. Using gloves, toss everything together. Transfer to a clean, quart-size (950 ml) jar and refrigerate overnight.

 MAKE AHEAD

THE KIMCHI WILL KEEP IN THE REFRIGERATOR FOR 2 WEEKS. THE LONGER IT SITS, THE FUNKIER THE SMELL.

VARIATION: Daikon Kimchi (kkakdugi) is another popular Korean *banchan,* or side dish. It's usually served with a dozen or so small plates at Korean restaurants. Made just like traditional kimchi, simply substitute 2 medium daikon, peeled and cut into ¾-inch (2 cm) cubes, for the Napa cabbage. Sprinkle with the salt and sugar, and refrigerate for 1 hour. Rinse and pat dry. Proceed with the recipe.

Korean Cubano

Ten hours may seem excessive for 2½ pounds (930 g) of usable meat, but believe me, it's well worth the wait. Start it at 8:00 a.m. and by dinnertime, well, a late dinnertime, it's done. You don't even actually need to cook it one go, but can, in a pinch, break it up over 2 days (8 hours the first day and 2 hours then next) as long as it reaches 195°F (91°C). Of course, there's always the option of buying precooked roasted pork, making this east-west sandwich super quick.

**MAKES
4 SANDWICHES**

➤ **ACTIVE: 15 MINUTES;
TOTAL: 30 MINUTES**

¼ cup (60 g) mayonnaise
4 soft hero rolls, split lengthwise
2 cups (300 g) Almost-Instant
   Kimchi
1 pound (455 g) shredded Korean-
   Spiced Roast Pork, recipe follows
½ cup (77 g) Spicy Bread-and-
   Butter Pickles (pg 21)
6 ounces (170 g) sliced Swiss
   cheese
Oil for brushing

1. Heat a panini press. Spread the mayonnaise on the bottom halves of the rolls and top with the Almost-Instant Kimchi. Divide the pork between the rolls, and top with the pickles and cheese. Close the sandwiches and brush lightly with oil.

2. Press the sandwiches in the panini press until the bread is golden and crisp and the cheese is melted, about 8 minutes. If you don't have a panini press, heat a large, cast-iron griddle. Place the sandwiches on the griddle and top with a baking sheet and several heavy pots. Cook over moderate heat until the bottom is crusty and golden, about 4 minutes. Flip and cook the other side. Cut each sandwich in half and serve right away.

Korean-Spiced Roast Pork

➤ **ACTIVE: 1 HOUR; TOTAL: 12 HOURS**

Low and slow is the only way to cook a pork shoulder. The fat gently melts into the meat making it exquisitely tender and succulent. The key is to cook the pork to 195°F (91°C), which may sound really high, but that's when the collagen begins to break down, giving the pork that melt-in-your-mouth texture.

MAKES 2½ POUNDS (930 G) SHREDDED PORK

10 garlic cloves

2 tablespoons (12 g) thinly sliced ginger

2 tablespoons (15 g) kochugaru (Korean pepper flakes)

1½ tablespoons (14 g) kosher salt

1 tablespoon (15 ml) Asian sesame oil

2 tablespoons (30 ml) canola oil

6-pound (2.7 kg) pork shoulder with skin

1. Preheat the oven to 250°F (120°C, or gas mark ½). In a mini food processor, combine the garlic, ginger, kochugaru, salt, sesame oil, and canola oil. Purée until fairly smooth.

2. Using a sharp paring knife, make deep slits into the pork all over and fill with the spice paste. Place the roast in a large, deep roasting pan, skin-side down. Fill with 1½ inches (3.5 cm) of water. Rub the remaining spice paste on the meat. Cover with foil and roast for 8 hours. Remove the foil, turn the roast skin-side up and roast, uncovered, until an instant-read thermometer inserted into the center registers 195°F (91°C), about 2 hours longer. Add water to the pan as necessary to avoid scorching. Raise the heat to 450°F (230°C, or gas mark 8) and roast 15 minutes, until the skin is crisp.

3. Let cool slightly, then, using gloved hands, remove the skin and pull the meat into large shreds, discarding excess fat. Pour off the fat from the roasting pan and stir a few spoonfuls of the pan drippings into the meat.

TIP: For delicious homemade pork cracklings, using scissors, cut the pork skin into ½-inch (1 cm)-wide strips. Heat ½ inch (1 cm) of oil in a medium skillet. Add the pork skin in batches, and cook over moderate heat, turning occasionally, until the skin is puffed, about 5 minutes. Drain on paper towels and sprinkle with salt. Mmmm!

Pickled Red Cabbage with Horseradish and Caraway

MAKES 1 PINT (475 ML)

➡️ **ACTIVE: 30 MINUTES; TOTAL: 30 MINUTES PLUS OVERNIGHT**

4 cups (280 g) thinly shredded red cabbage (half of a 1-pound cabbage)

¼ cup (60 g) coarsely shredded horseradish

2 tablespoons (18 g) kosher salt

1 teaspoon yellow mustard seeds

1 teaspoon caraway seeds

¼ cup (28 g) dried currants

¾ cup (175 ml) distilled white vinegar

½ cup (100 g) sugar

Not sure if this is Russian or Irish, but the flavors of caraway and currants are reminiscent of both pumpernickel and soda bread.

1. In a large bowl, combine the cabbage, horseradish, and salt, and squeeze/pulse with your hands for about 1 minute until wilted. Let sit for 10 minutes, then rinse under cold running water. Squeeze out the excess water and return to the bowl. Add the mustard seeds, caraway seeds, and currants. Pack the mixture into a clean, pint-size (475 ml) jar.

2. In a small, nonreactive saucepan, combine the vinegar and sugar. Bring to a boil. Pour the hot brine into the jar, seal, and let cool at room temperature. Refrigerate overnight.

MAKE AHEAD

THE PICKLES WILL KEEP IN THE REFRIGERATOR FOR 4 WEEKS.

⸘ USES FOR PICKLED CABBAGE:

• instead of sauerkraut, use as hot dog topper,
• Reuben,
• pastrami on rye

Grilled Gruyére with Pickled Red Cabbage

Be sure to squeeze the excess liquid from the cabbage to keep your sandwich from getting soggy.

MAKES 1 SANDWICH

 ACTIVE: 15 MINUTES; TOTAL: 15 MINUTES

2 slices multigrain sandwich bread

4 teaspoons (18 g) unsalted butter, softened

2 tablespoons (10 g) grated Parmigiano-Reggiano

1 teaspoon Dijon mustard

3 ounces (85 g) sliced Gruyère

3 tablespoons (28 g) Pickled Red Cabbage with Horseradish and Caraway, squeezed

1. On a work surface, spread both slices of bread with the butter on one side only. Sprinkle the Parmesan cheese over the butter, and press lightly to adhere. Invert the bread, and spread each slice with the mustard. On 1 slice, add half of the Gruyère, followed by the cabbage and remaining Gruyère. Top with the bread, Parmesan side out, and press slightly.

2. Place the sandwich on an ungreased nonstick skillet. Cover and cook over low heat until the Gruyère is melted and the bread is browned on the outside, about 8 minutes, turning once. Transfer to a plate, cut in half, and serve right away.

Giardiniera
(Mixed Italian Pickles)

ACTIVE: 30 MINUTES; TOTAL: 30 MINUTES PLUS OVERNIGHT

Most commercial giardinieras use straight vinegar, but I've added a bit of olive oil to balance the tartness and make this more like a pickled veggie salad. If you can't find shishito peppers or baby bell peppers, ½-inch (1 cm) strips of red bell peppers will do the trick.

MAKES 2 QUARTS (ABOUT 1.9 L)

- 4 ounces (115 g) shishito or baby bell peppers
- 4 carrots, cut into ¼ x 1½-inch (6 cm x 3.5 cm) matchsticks
- 4 celery ribs, preferably center, thinly sliced
- 4 cups (12 ounces, or 340 g) 1-inch cauliflower florets
- ¼ cup plus 2 tablespoons (56 g) kosher salt
- 1 teaspoon coriander seeds
- 1 teaspoon whole peppercorns
- 2 bay leaves
- 1 cup (235 ml) pure olive oil
- 2 cups (475 ml) distilled white vinegar
- 1 cup (235 ml) water
- 2 teaspoons (4 g) dried oregano, crumbled

1. Poke the peppers all over with a skewer. Place them into a large, tall glass or plastic container. Add the carrots, celery, and cauliflower. In a large bowl, combine the salt, coriander seeds, peppercorns, and bay leaves with 6 cups (1.4 L) of water. Stir until the salt is dissolved. Pour the brine over the vegetables, and top with a small plate to keep them submerged. Cover with plastic and refrigerate overnight.

2. Drain the vegetables, rinsing briefly and shake out the excess liquid. Pack the vegetables into 2 clean, quart-size (950 ml) jars, and add ½ cup (118 ml) of oil to each jar. In a small, nonreactive saucepan, combine the vinegar, water, and oregano. Bring to a boil. Pour the hot liquid into the jars, seal, and let cool at room temperature. Refrigerate overnight.

MAKE AHEAD

THE PICKLES WILL KEEP IN THE REFRIGERATOR FOR 2 WEEKS.

Fire-Roasted Pickled Baby Bell Peppers

ACTIVE: 45 MINUTES; TOTAL: 45 MINUTES PLUS OVERNIGHT

The idea of roasting and peeling a pound of baby bell peppers can be daunting. (I don't blame you—these babies are just so cute.) This pickle will work just as well with roasted, full-size peppers cut into strips before pickling.

MAKES 2 PINTS (950 ML)

1 pound (164 g) baby bell peppers
2 garlic cloves, sliced
1 tablespoon (6 g) fennel seeds
½ teaspoon whole black peppercorns
½ cup (120 ml) distilled white vinegar
½ cup (120 ml) water
1½ tablespoons (14 g) kosher salt
1½ tablespoons (20 g) sugar

1. Roast the peppers on a hot grill or under a broiler, turning, until charred and softened, about 10 minutes. Transfer the peppers to a bowl, cover with plastic, and let cool, about 20 minutes. Peel the peppers under running water, removing as much of the skin as possible.

2. Divide the peppers, garlic, fennel seeds, and peppercorns between 2 clean, pint-size (475 ml) jars.

3. In a small, nonreactive saucepan, combine the vinegar, water, salt, and sugar. Bring to a boil. Pour the hot brine into the jars, seal, and let cool at room temperature. Refrigerate overnight.

MAKE AHEAD

THE PICKLES WILL KEEP IN THE REFRIGERATOR FOR 4 WEEKS.

Pickled-Pepper Romesco

I often make this Romesco, a Spanish sauce using fried bread, toasted almonds, and *piquillo* peppers, which can be expensive and difficult to find. Pickled peppers are wonderful here—the texture is very similar and the brine adds a splash of acid.

MAKES 2 CUPS (475 ML)

TOTAL: 20 MINUTES

¾ cup (175 ml) extra-virgin olive oil, divided
1 cup diced (½ inch, or 1 cm) sourdough bread
2 garlic cloves, thickly sliced
1 can (14 ounces, or 397 g) diced tomatoes, drained and pressed dry (1 cup)
⅔ cup (89 g) Fire-Roasted Pickled Baby Bell Peppers, plus 2 tablespoons (28 ml) brine, divided; peppers are stemmed and seeded
¼ cup plus 2 tablespoons (52 g) roasted, salted almonds (smoked preferably)
Salt and freshly ground pepper

1. In a medium skillet, heat ½ cup (120 ml) of the oil until shimmering. Add the bread and cook over moderate heat, stirring until lightly golden, about 4 minutes. Add the garlic and cook, stirring, until the garlic is golden and the bread deeply toasted. Using a slotted spoon, transfer the bread and garlic to a mini food processor.

2. Off the heat, carefully add the tomatoes and pickled peppers. Cook, stirring, until lightly caramelized about 5 minutes. Scrape the mixture, including the oil into the food processor. Add the almonds and the 2 tablespoons (28 ml) brine. Purée to a chunky paste. Add the remaining ¼ cup (55 ml) olive oil and purée until smooth. Season with salt and pepper.

MAKE AHEAD

THE ROMESCO CAN BE REFRIGERATED FOR UP TO 2 WEEKS.

﹥ Serving Suggestions for Pickled-Pepper Romesco:

- Pickled Leeks and Asparagus;
- grilled bread with cheese;
- grilled fish,
- steaks,
- pork,
- shrimp,
- or chicken

Pickled Red and Green Chiles

➡️ **ACTIVE: 20 MINUTES; TOTAL: 20 MINUTES PLUS OVERNIGHT**

I'd always thought that pickled jalapeños were difficult to make, opting for the canned ones from Mexico. The can is so colorful and the quality is quite nice, but nothing compares to these homemade pickled chiles. They stay crisp for a really long time, making them especially easy to slice. I use them on everything—tacos, pizza, sandwiches, salsa, pasta . . . you name it.

**MAKES 1 PINT
(475 ML)**

4 medium jalapeños
4 medium red Fresno chiles
2 sprigs (2 inches, or 5 cm, each)
    oregano
1 large garlic clove, sliced
1 teaspoon whole coriander seeds
½ teaspoon whole cumin seeds
½ cup (120 ml) distilled white
    vinegar
½ cup (120 ml) water
1 tablespoon (9 g) kosher salt
1 teaspoon sugar

1. Prick the chiles several times with a toothpick. Put the oregano, garlic, coriander seeds, and cumin seeds into a clean, pint-size (475 ml) jar. Pack the chiles into the jar.

2. In a small, nonreactive saucepan, combine the vinegar, water, salt, and sugar. Bring to a boil. Pour the hot brine into the jar, seal, and let cool at room temperature. Refrigerate overnight.

**MAKE
AHEAD**

THE PICKLES WILL
KEEP IN THE
REFRIGERATOR FOR
2 MONTHS.

➤ TIP: Purée the chiles, garlic, and (strained) brine for a super-tangy hot sauce.

Tangy Green Tomato Pickles

MAKES 2 PINTS (950 ML)

➡ **ACTIVE: 30 MINUTES; TOTAL: 1½ HOURS PLUS OVERNIGHT**

As a kid, my folks would take us to Brody's, a kosher deli, for matzo ball soup, pastrami sandwiches, and the best hot dogs on the planet. The pickle tray, a staple at kosher delis, came with dills, sours, half-sours, and pickled green tomatoes, which I always avoided. As an Italian, the idea of anything but a ripe, red tomato was anathema. Plus they were whole and looked wholly unappealing. I've come to love green tomatoes and wanted to include a recipe, but still couldn't bring myself to pickle them whole. Here, they're sliced and prepared much like the other sliced cucumber pickles in this chapter. Great on sandwiches, in salads, added to coleslaws, on burgers, or anywhere you'd add pickles.

3 large green tomatoes (unripe—not heirloom), cored
1 large jalapeño
2 large garlic cloves, thinly sliced
2 tablespoons (18 g) kosher salt
1½ teaspoons coriander seeds
1½ teaspoons yellow mustard seeds
1½ teaspoons whole black peppercorns
8 sprigs (2 inches, or 5 cm, each) dill
2 bay leaves, preferably Turkish
¾ cup (175 ml) distilled white vinegar
¾ cup (175 ml) water

1. Using a mandolin, slice the tomatoes and jalapeño ⅛-inch (3 mm) thick. Place the tomatoes, jalapeño, and garlic in a colander set in a bowl, and toss with the salt. Place a plate and heavy can on top and refrigerate for 1 hour. Pour off the liquid and soak the tomatoes, jalapeño, and garlic in ice water for 10 minutes. Drain and pat dry. The tomatoes should still be a bit salty. Wipe out the bowl.

2. Return the tomatoes, jalapeño, and garlic to the bowl along with the coriander seeds, mustard seeds, peppercorns, dill, and bay leaves. Toss to combine. Pack 2 clean, pint-size (475 ml) jars with the mixture.

3. In a small, nonreactive saucepan, combine the vinegar and water. Bring to a boil. Pour the hot brine into the jars, seal, and let cool at room temperature. Refrigerate overnight.

MAKE AHEAD

THE PICKLES WILL KEEP IN THE REFRIGERATOR FOR 2 WEEKS.

Pickled Wild Mushrooms

MAKES 1½ PINTS (710 ML)

➤ **ACTIVE: 30 MINUTES; TOTAL: 30 MINUTES PLUS OVERNIGHT**

¾ cup (175 ml) extra-virgin olive oil

1 pound (455 g) mixed wild mushrooms, such as shiitake (caps), oyster, cremini, maitake, chanterelle, cleaned and thickly sliced (8 cups)

3 garlic cloves, sliced

3 sprigs (3 inches, or 7.5 cm, each) rosemary

3 small bay leaves, preferably Turkish

1½ teaspoons cracked black peppercorns

1 teaspoon kosher salt

¾ cup (175 ml) white wine vinegar

I haven't met a mushroom I don't love, and any will work here. But, if you plan on using portobellos, be sure to remove the black gills from the underside of the mushrooms. Use a spoon and scrape them away.

1. In a large, nonstick skillet, heat the oil until shimmering. Add the mushrooms, garlic, rosemary, and bay leaves. Cook over moderate heat, stirring occasionally until the mushrooms are tender and browned, 10 to 12 minutes. Add the pepper and salt, and cook 1 minute longer. Add the vinegar and bring to a boil. Simmer over low heat for 2 minutes.

2. Using a slotted spoon, transfer the mixture to 3 clean, ½-pint (235 ml) jars. Ladle the hot dressing on top, seal, and let cool at room temperature. Refrigerate overnight.

MAKE AHEAD

THE PICKLES WILL KEEP IN THE REFRIGERATOR FOR 4 WEEKS.

➣ USES FOR PICKLED MUSHROOMS

- *Mushroom Risotto*—stir drained pickled mushrooms into risotto at the end
- *Mushroom-Avocado Tartine*—rub toasted sourdough with garlic, top with mashed avocado and pickled mushrooms
- *Steak with Mushrooms and Blue Cheese*—after pan-frying steak, quickly sauté drained pickled mushrooms, and spoon over steak, and garnish with crumbled blue cheese
- *Wild Mushroom Bread Salad*—toss pickled mushrooms with toasted rustic bread, shaved ricotta salata, halved cherry tomatoes, and some of the pickling liquid
- *Wild Mushroom Panini*—layer drained pickled mushrooms, fontina, and grainy mustard between sliced sourdough, and press in a panini press

Wilted Kale Salad with Bacon and Pickled Mushrooms

The combination of pickled mushrooms, smoky bacon, kale, and garlicky croutons is divine in this riff on the classic Frisée aux Lardons. The dressing, a tiny bit of bacon fat, and the pickle brine replace the oil and vinegar found in most vinaigrettes.

 ACTIVE: 20 MINUTES; TOTAL: 20 MINUTES

4 cups (268 g) thinly sliced stemmed kale
Sea salt
4 slices thick-cut bacon, cut into ½-inch (1 cm) pieces
½ cup (112 g) well-drained Pickled Wild Mushrooms, plus 2 tablespoons (28 ml) of the brine, divided
Freshly ground pepper
1 cup (40 g) toasted garlic croutons
Shaved Parmegiano-Reggiano, for serving

1. In a large serving bowl, toss the kale with a pinch of salt. Squeeze lightly to wilt.

2. In a medium skillet, cook the bacon over moderately high heat until browned and crisp, 5 to 6 minutes. Using a slotted spoon, transfer the bacon to the kale and discard all but 1 tablespoon (15 ml) of the bacon fat in the pan. Add the mushrooms to the skillet, season with pepper, and cook over moderately high heat until slightly browned, about 5 minutes. Off the heat, add the brine. Immediately pour the mixture over the kale, and toss to coat. Add the croutons and cheese, and toss again. Serve right away.

Fruit Pickles

Bourbon-Pickled Blackberries

ACTIVE: 30 MINUTES; TOTAL: 30 MINUTES PLUS OVERNIGHT

I love the brandy cherries from France that you find in high-end cocktail lounges and really wanted to try this with blackberries. The sweet and sour brine is elevated with a splash of bourbon, making this pickle particularly delicious in drinks and desserts.

MAKES 2 PINTS (950 ML)

¾ cup (150 g) sugar

1 teaspoon cracked black peppercorns

4 strips (2 inches, or 5 cm, each) orange zest removed with vegetable peeler, divided

¾ cup (175 ml) distilled white vinegar

¼ cup plus 2 tablespoons (88 ml) water

¼ cup (60 ml) bourbon

2 pints (300 g) firm-but-ripe blackberries

1. In a small, nonreactive saucepan, using a wooden spoon, mash the sugar with the black peppercorns and 2 orange zest strips until the sugar is slightly colored. Add the vinegar and water. Bring to a boil. Cover and let sit for 10 minutes.

2. Pack the berries and remaining 2 orange zest strips into 2 clean, pint-size (475 ml) jars. Return the brine to a boil. Strain the brine into the jars, seal, and let cool at room temperature. Refrigerate overnight.

MAKE AHEAD

THE PICKLES WILL KEEP IN THE REFRIGERATOR FOR 4 WEEKS.

⇒ USES FOR PICKLED BLACKBERRIES:

• Add some berries and a bit of the brine to your favorite daiquiri or fruit salad;

• serve with shortcakes and sweetened cream;

• garnish for pound cake;

• purée berries and brine, and freeze for sorbet;

• mash and stir into lemonade.

Blackberry Pickle Gin Smash

TOTAL: 5 MINUTES

4 Bourbon-Pickled Blackberries
1 small lemon wedge
2 ounces (60 ml) brine
1 ounce (28 ml) gin
Ice
Club soda

Totally refreshing, this was my summer go-to cocktail.

In a cocktail shaker, muddle the blackberries with the lemon wedge. Add the brine, gin, and ice. Shake well. Strain the mixture into an ice-filled rocks glass, and top with a splash of soda.

Blackberry Pickle Eton Mess

Eton mess is an English dessert originating from Eton College where it was served at the annual cricket game against a rival school. Strawberries and bananas were traditional, but I like this with juicy, pickled blackberries. Using store-bought meringues makes this an almost-instant dessert.

MAKES 4 SERVINGS

 TOTAL: 15 MINUTES

6 large meringue cookies (Miss Meringue) (2½ ounces, or 121 g)

1 cup (235 ml) heavy cream, chilled

2 tablespoons (15 g) confectioners' sugar

¾ cup (110 g) strained Bourbon-Pickled Blackberries, plus ¼ cup (60 ml) brine, divided

1. Coarsely crumble the cookies and place one-third in 4 wine glasses.

2. In a chilled bowl, whip the cream with the confectioners' sugar to soft peaks. Lightly crush the berries (reserving 4 for the garnish), and fold them into the cream. Spoon half of the mixture into the glasses, followed by another layer of meringues and the remaining cream. Top with the remaining meringues, and drizzle each with a tablespoon of the brine. Garnish with the whole blackberries and serve right away.

⟩ **TIP:** For a quick English trifle, substitute 4 slices of pound cake, cut into ½-inch (1 cm) cubes, for the meringue cookies.

White Balsamic Pickled Strawberries

These sweet and tangy berries are lovely with soft cheeses such as fromage blanc, Camembert, or chèvre. Drizzle some of the brine on top, and serve with golden, buttery toast points. Equally delicious with shortcakes and whipped cream, mashed into lemonade, or puréed into daiquiris.

MAKES 1 PINT (475 ML)

1 tablespoon (6 g) whole fennel seeds

¾ cup (175 ml) water

¼ cup plus 2 tablespoons (88 ml) white balsamic vinegar

¼ cup (50 g) sugar

½ teaspoon lavender (Alternatively, use herbes de Provence.)

12 ounces (340 g) small strawberries, stemmed, halved if large

1 strip (4 inches, or 10 cm) lemon zest removed with a vegetable peeler, finely julienned

1. In a small, nonreactive saucepan, toast the fennel seeds over moderate heat until fragrant, about 1 minute. Add the water, vinegar, sugar, and lavender. Bring to a boil. Cover and let sit for 10 minutes.

2. Pack the berries and lemon zest into a clean, pint-size (475 ml) jar. Return the brine to a boil. Strain the brine into the jar, seal, and let cool at room temperature. Refrigerate overnight.

MAKE AHEAD

THE PICKLES WILL KEEP IN THE REFRIGERATOR FOR 4 WEEKS.

TIP: Fold 1 tablespoon (10 g) chopped crystallized ginger into sweetened whipped crème fraîche, and serve with pickled strawberries.

Chai-Pickled Peaches

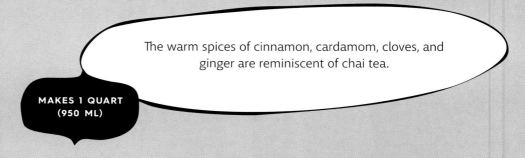

The warm spices of cinnamon, cardamom, cloves, and ginger are reminiscent of chai tea.

MAKES 1 QUART (950 ML)

 ACTIVE: 30 MINUTES; TOTAL: 30 MINUTES PLUS OVERNIGHT

1 cup (235 ml) distilled white vinegar
1 cup (235 ml) water
2 tablespoons (16 g) grated fresh ginger
2 tablespoons (8 g) green cardamom pods
1 tablespoon (4 g) whole cloves
1 tablespoon (5 g) cracked peppercorns
2 cinnamon sticks
¾ cup (150 g) sugar
1½ pounds (680 g) firm, slightly under-ripe peaches

1. In a medium, nonreactive saucepan, combine the vinegar, water, ginger, cardamom, cloves, peppercorns, and cinnamon sticks. Bring to a boil. Cover and let sit off the heat for 20 minutes. Add the sugar and return to a boil.

2. Meanwhile, peel the peaches with a vegetable peeler and cut each into eighths. Pack the peaches into a clean, quart-size (950 ml) jar. Strain the brine into the jar, seal, and let cool at room temperature. Refrigerate overnight.

MAKE AHEAD

THE PICKLES WILL KEEP IN THE REFRIGERATOR FOR 4 WEEKS.

Toasted Pound Cake with Chai-Pickled Peaches

MAKES 4 SERVINGS

As if peaches and cream isn't enough, the pound cake is dipped in sugar and caramelized in a skillet for a crispy, almost crème brûlée crackle top.

 TOTAL: 15 MINUTES

2 tablespoons (26 g) sugar
4 slices (1 inch, or 2.5 cm, thick) pound cake
2 tablespoons (28 g) unsalted butter
4 ounces (115 g) cream cheese, softened
1 tablespoon (8 g) confectioners' sugar
1 tablespoon (10 g) minced crystallized ginger
1 cup (170 g) Chai-Pickled Peaches, sliced; plus 3 tablespoons (45 ml) brine, divided
¼ cup (30 g) chopped toasted almonds

1. Spread the sugar on a plate. Press each side of the pound cake into the sugar. In a large, nonstick skillet, melt the butter. Add the pound cake and cook over moderate heat, turning once, until the sugar is caramelized, 1 to 2 minutes. Transfer to plates and let cool slightly.

2. In a small mixing bowl, using a handheld electric mixer, combine the cream cheese, confectioners' sugar, ginger, and brine. Beat on medium speed until smooth.

3. Divide the peaches between the plates, and top with the cream cheese mixture. Garnish with the almonds and serve right away.

Pickled Plums

Sweet and sour, smoky and spicy, these pickled plums are so versatile, they can be used with savory dishes, such as sautéed pork with plums, or with desserts, such as fruit salads.

MAKES 2 PINTS (950 ML)

¾ cup (175 ml) distilled white vinegar

½ cup (120 ml) water

¾ cup (150 g) sugar

1 dried smoked serrano or dried chipotle chile (or scant ½ teaspoon chipotle powder)

1 teaspoon whole black peppercorns

2 bay leaves, preferably Turkish

5 firm-but-ripe red or purple plums, (1¼ pounds, or 570 g), halved and thinly sliced

1. In a small, nonreactive saucepan, combine the vinegar, water, sugar, serrano chile, peppercorns, and bay leaves. Bring to a boil. Cover and let sit 20 minutes.

2. Pack the plums into 2 clean, pint-size (475 ml) jars. Return the brine to a boil, and strain into the jars. Seal and let cool at room temperature. Refrigerate overnight.

MAKE AHEAD

THE PICKLES WILL KEEP IN THE REFRIGERATOR FOR 4 WEEKS.

Pickled Plum Granita

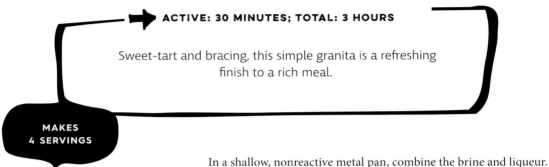

ACTIVE: 30 MINUTES; TOTAL: 3 HOURS

Sweet-tart and bracing, this simple granita is a refreshing finish to a rich meal.

MAKES 4 SERVINGS

1¼ cups (295 ml) brine from
   Pickled Plums (strained)
2 tablespoons mirabelle (plum
   eau-de-vie) or white rum
Pickled Plums for garnish (optional)

In a shallow, nonreactive metal pan, combine the brine and liqueur. Freeze for 30 minutes. Scrape the frozen crystals that have formed around the edges into the center and return to the freezer. Continue freezing and scraping every 30 minutes until the ice crystals are flaky, fluffy, and frozen, about 3 hours total. Scoop into small bowls and garnish with pickled plums, if desired.

GRANITA OPTIONS: watermelon brine, pickled cherry brine, pickled pineapple brine, or bourbon-pickled blackberry brine.

Honey and Star Anise Pickled Apricots

Apricots are around for such a short time,
I like to take full advantage of the season. Look for ripe,
but firm, apricots.

**MAKES 1½ PINTS
(710 ML)**

 ACTIVE: 30 MINUTES; TOTAL: 30 MINUTES PLUS OVERNIGHT

1 cup (235 ml) distilled white
   vinegar
⅓ cup (80 ml) water
⅓ cup (66 g) sugar
⅓ cup (115 g) honey
2 star anise, broken
2 teaspoons (4 g) cracked black
   peppercorns
1¼ pounds (570 g) firm apricots,
   halved

1. In a small, nonreactive saucepan, combine the vinegar, water, sugar, honey, star anise, and peppercorns. Bring to a boil. Cover and let sit for 20 minutes.

2. Pack the apricots into 3 clean, ½-pint (235 ml) jars. Return the brine to a boil, and strain into the jars. Seal and let cool at room temperature. Refrigerate overnight.

**MAKE
AHEAD**

THE PICKLES WILL
KEEP IN THE
REFRIGERATOR FOR
4 WEEKS.

Pickled Apricot BBQ Glaze for Ribs

**MAKES 1 CUP (250 G)
(ENOUGH FOR
2 RACKS OF RIBS)**

**ACTIVE: 10 MINUTES;
TOTAL: 15 MINUTES
PLUS GRILLING TIME FOR
THE RIBS**

1 tablespoon (14 g) unsalted butter
¼ cup (40 g) minced sweet onion
¾ cup (128 g) Honey and Star
  Anise Pickled Apricots, coarsely
  chopped; plus ½ cup (120 ml)
  brine, divided
2 tablespoons (30 g) light brown
  sugar
1 tablespoon (15 g) Dijon mustard
¼ teaspoon cayenne pepper
Salt
2 racks cooked St. Louis–cut
  spareribs, on the grill

Tucked away in the back of the pantry growing up, there was always a jar of Saucy Susan, a peach-apricot sauce that my mom used to glaze pork chops or chicken drumsticks. It was never as good as it promised, which probably accounted for it being at the *back* of the pantry. This version, using pickled apricots, caramelized onion, and a bit of the tart brine, is everything I'd hoped for from Saucy Susan. This is great on ribs, but try it on grilled chicken, pork chops, or turkey burgers.

1. In a medium saucepan, melt the butter. Add the onion and cook over moderate heat, stirring occasionally, until softened and lightly browned, about 6 minutes. Add the chopped apricots. Cook until just slightly broken down, about 3 minutes. Add the brine, brown sugar, mustard, and cayenne. Bring to a simmer. Transfer the mixture to a blender, and purée until smooth. Return the mixture to the saucepan, season with salt, and simmer until reduced to 1 cup (250 g), about 5 minutes longer.

2. Brush the fully cooked ribs with the glaze and grill, turning and brushing until lightly caramelized all over, about 10 minutes. Cut into individual ribs and serve.

Pickled Black Cherries with Cardamom

MAKES ABOUT 1 QUART (950 ML)

Don't be tempted to pack the cherries into a pint-size (475 ml) jar. You'll need a quart-size (950 ml) jar to fit all the liquid which is an amazing by-product of these fruity, luscious, pickled cherries. Use it in vinaigrettes, cocktails, or granitas. Boil it down slightly and pour over ice cream, or use as a bbq glaze for ribs.

 ACTIVE: 45 MINUTES; TOTAL: 45 MINUTES PLUS OVERNIGHT

½ cup (120 ml) balsamic vinegar

¼ cup (60 ml) distilled white vinegar

¾ cup (175 ml) water

¾ cup (150 g) sugar

2 slices (quarter-size, or 25 mm diameter by 2 mm thick) peeled ginger

2 strips (2 inches, or 10 cm, each) orange zest removed with vegetable peeler

1 tablespoon (4 g) cardamom pods, lightly bruised

1 pound (455 g) black cherries, stemmed and pitted

1. In a small, nonreactive saucepan, combine the balsamic vinegar, distilled white vinegar, water, sugar, ginger, orange zest, and cardamom. Bring to a boil.

2. Pack the cherries into a clean, quart-size (950 ml) jar. Pour the hot brine into the jar, seal, and let cool at room temperature. Refrigerate overnight.

MAKE AHEAD

THE PICKLES WILL KEEP IN THE REFRIGERATOR FOR 4 WEEKS.

Duck Breasts with Pickled Cherries

Duck with cherries is a French classic. This reimagined brasserie favorite uses pickled cherries in place of fresh. The brine adds a sweet-tart balance to the rich sauce. (Bonus—save the rendered duck fat to fry par-cooked potatoes.)

MAKES 4 SERVINGS

 TOTAL: 25 MINUTES

4 white Peking duck breasts, about 8 ounces (225 g) each
1 teaspoon canola oil
Salt and freshly ground pepper
1 medium shallot, minced
2 thyme sprigs
1 cup (245 g) Pickled Black Cherries, halved, plus ½ cup (120 ml) strained brine, divided
½ cup (120 ml) dry red wine, such as cabernet sauvignon
1 tablespoon (14 g) unsalted butter

1. Pound the duck lightly between sheets of plastic to an even thickness. Rub the skin with the oil and using a sharp knife, make ¼-inch (6 mm) deep slashes in the skin in a cross-hatch pattern. Don't slice through the skin into the flesh. Season the duck all over with salt and pepper.

2. Heat a skillet over moderate heat and add the duck, skin-side down. Cook over moderate heat without disturbing for 12 minutes, until the skin is deeply golden. Spoon off the fat as it is rendered. (Reserve it for another use—it will keep in the refrigerator for months.) Raise the heat to medium-high and cook for 15 seconds. Flip the duck and cook until browned, about 2 minutes for medium-cooked duck.

3. Transfer the duck breasts to a plate while you make the sauce. Pour off all but 1 tablespoon (15 ml) fat from the pan, add the shallots and thyme, and cook until softened, 1 minute. Add the brine and wine. Bring to a boil. Simmer, scraping up any browned bits stuck to the pan, until the liquid is reduced by two-thirds, about 10 minutes. Add the cherries and bring to a boil. Add the butter and swirl to combine.

4. Slice each duck breast and place on plates. Spoon the sauce on top and serve.

Pickled Figs with Balsamic

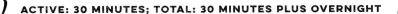
ACTIVE: 30 MINUTES; TOTAL: 30 MINUTES PLUS OVERNIGHT

**MAKES 1 PINT
(475 ML)**

12 small green figs (about 10
ounces, or 280 g)
½ cup (120 ml) white balsamic
vinegar
½ cup (120 ml) water
½ cup (100 g) sugar
4 strips (2 inches, or 5 cm, each)
lemon zest removed with
vegetable peeler, finely julienned

Green figs are lovely here, but they're not always available.
Brown Turkey figs are easier to find and just as yummy. You'll
want to use regular balsamic vinegar for the brine. Either
way, the figs are delicious, and the brine is amazing for use
in vinaigrettes, or deglazing sautéed pork chops, or drizzled
over ripe cheese. Serve the figs as part of a charcuterie platter with cheeses, salumi, and roasted nuts.

1. Pierce the figs several times with a
skewer.

2. In a medium, nonreactive saucepan, combine the vinegar, water, sugar,
and lemon zest. Bring to a boil. Add the
figs and simmer for 5 minutes. Spoon
the figs into a clean, pint-size (475 ml)
jar and cover with the brine. Seal and
let cool at room temperature. Refrigerate overnight.

**MAKE
AHEAD**

THE PICKELS WILL
KEEP IN THE
REFRIGERATOR FOR
4 WEEKS.

Bacon-Wrapped Pickled Figs and Goat Cheese

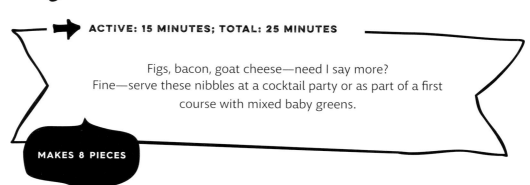

ACTIVE: 15 MINUTES; TOTAL: 25 MINUTES

Figs, bacon, goat cheese—need I say more?
Fine—serve these nibbles at a cocktail party or as part of a first
course with mixed baby greens.

MAKES 8 PIECES

8 slices bacon
8 Pickled Figs, plus 2 tablespoons
   (28 ml) brine, divided
4 tablespoons (38 g) fresh goat
   cheese
Toothpicks

1. Preheat the oven to 400°F (200°C, or gas mark 6) and line a small baking sheet with parchment.

2. Cook the bacon in a large skillet, turning once, until lightly browned but not crisp, about 6 minutes. Drain on paper towels.

3. Using a sharp knife, cut the figs almost in half, starting at the stem end but not going all the way through. Divide the cheese evenly and fill the figs. Wrap each in a piece of bacon, securing with a decorative pick, and transfer to the baking sheet. Bake until the bacon is crisp and the cheese is soft, about 5 minutes. Transfer to a platter, and drizzle with some of the brine. Serve hot or warm.

Pickled Grapes with Vanilla and Pink Peppercorns

These pickled grapes are yummy as part of a charcuterie platter with hard and soft cheeses, roasted nuts, and cured meats. They are also delicious when added to a skillet after sautéing pork or chicken.

MAKES 1 QUART (950 ML)

ACTIVE: 30 MINUTES; TOTAL: 30 MINUTES PLUS OVERNIGHT

1 cup (235 ml) distilled white vinegar

1 cup (235 ml) water

¾ cup (150 g) sugar

½ plump vanilla bean, halved and seeds scraped

4 cups (600 g) red or green seedless grapes, stemmed

8 green cardamom pods, lightly crushed

1 tablespoon (5 g) pink peppercorns

1. In a small, nonreactive saucepan, combine the vinegar, water, sugar, and vanilla bean seeds. Bring to a boil.

2. Pack the grapes, cardamom, peppercorns, and scraped vanilla pod into a clean, quart-size (950 ml) jar. Pour the hot brine into the jar, seal, and let cool at room temperature. Refrigerate overnight.

MAKE AHEAD

THE PICKELS WILL KEEP IN THE REFRIGERATOR FOR 2 WEEKS.

Easy Grape Sorbet

Sweet and tangy, this sorbet is super refreshing, especially on a hot day. Scoop some into champagne flutes, and top with sparkling wine or sangria for a brilliant cocktail.

MAKES 4 SERVINGS

 ACTIVE: 15 MINUTES; TOTAL: 4 HOURS

2 cups (300 g) Pickled Grapes, plus
  ¾ cup (175 ml) strained brine
2 tablespoons (28 ml) lemon juice
⅓ cup (66 g) sugar

In a blender, combine the grapes, brine, lemon juice, and sugar. Purée until smooth. Strain the mixture through a fine-mesh sieve, and transfer to a shallow, nonreactive metal pan. Freeze for 30 minutes. Scrape the frozen crystals that have formed around the edges into the center, and return to the freezer. Continue freezing and scraping every 30 minutes until the ice crystals are flaky, fluffy, and frozen, about 3 hours total. Scoop into small bowls.

Crunchy Pickled Pears with Warm Spices

MAKES 1 PINT (475 ML)

With a heady infusion of the sweet, wintery spices, cinnamon, cloves, and allspice, these pickled pears are especially delicious with cheeses and cured meats as part of a charcuterie platter, or added to salads, or stirred into sweetened oatmeal.

 ACTIVE: 30 MINUTES; TOTAL: 30 MINUTES PLUS OVERNIGHT

½ cup (120 ml) distilled white vinegar
¾ cup (175 ml) water
¼ cup plus 2 tablespoons (76 g) sugar
¼ teaspoon kosher salt
1 cinnamon stick, cracked
½ teaspoon whole cloves
½ teaspoon allspice berries
2 small Bosc pears (8 ounces, or 225 g), stemmed, cored, and cut into thin wedges

1. In a small, nonreactive saucepan, combine the vinegar, water, sugar, and salt. Bring to a boil.

2. Put the cinnamon, cloves, and allspice into a clean, pint-size (475 ml) jar, and add the pears. Pour the brine into the jar, seal, and let cool at room temperature. Refrigerate overnight.

MAKE AHEAD

BEST USED WITHIN 1 WEEK, THE PICKLES WILL KEEP IN THE REFRIGERATOR FOR UP TO 2 WEEKS.

Baked Camembert with Pickled Pears

The crunchy pears and toasted hazelnuts transform this simple dish into a spectacular first course. Use the pears and bread to scoop up the gooey melted cheese.

MAKES 6 SERVINGS

1 round (8 ounces, or 250 g) Camembert

1 tablespoon (15 ml) cognac

½ pint (235 ml) Crunchy Pickled Pears, plus 1 tablespoon (15 ml) brine, divided

¼ cup (28 g) toasted chopped hazelnuts

6 slices Danish rye bread, cut into rectangles, for serving

Preheat the oven to 400°F (200°C, or gas mark 6). Put the Camembert in a small shallow baking dish. Drizzle the cognac and brine over the cheese, and bake for 6 to 7 minutes, until the cheese is very soft. Spoon any liquid over the cheese, and sprinkle with the hazelnuts. Serve with the pickled pears and bread.

Pickled Lychees with Ginger and Lemongrass

Fresh lychees, floral and juicy, are probably my favorite tropical fruit. Unfortunately, they're only available for a few weeks in June and July. Lychees canned in their juice are the best alternative.

MAKES 1 PINT (475 ML)

➡ **ACTIVE: 30 MINUTES; TOTAL: 30 MINUTES PLUS OVERNIGHT**

¼ cup plus 2 tablespoons (88 ml) unseasoned rice vinegar

½ cup plus 2 tablespoons (148 ml) water

2 tablespoons (26 g) sugar

12 ounces (340 g) fresh lychees, peeled

1 piece (1 inch, or 2.5 cm) fresh ginger, peeled and finely julienned (about 1 tablespoon [8 g])

1 stalk (6 inches, or 15 cm) lemongrass, lightly bruised

3 sprigs (2 inches, or 5 cm, each) thyme sprigs

⌇ PICKLE SPRITZERS

Add a few tablespoons (45 ml) of sweet, fruit pickle brines to seltzer. Try Pickled Lychees, Pickled Pineapple, Pickled Plums, or Bourbon-Pickled Blackberries.

1. In a small, nonreactive saucepan, combine the vinegar, water, and sugar. Bring to a boil.

2. Pack the lychees, ginger, lemongrass, and thyme into a clean, pint-size (475 ml) jar. Pour the hot brine into the jar, seal, and let cool at room temperature. Refrigerate overnight.

MAKE AHEAD

THE PICKLES WILL KEEP IN THE REFRIGERATOR FOR 2 WEEKS.

Coconut-Lychee Ice Cream

Coconut and lychee is a heavenly tropical combination. Pickled lychees are folded into softened ice cream, then garnished with toasted coconut and macadamia nuts. The microwave does most of the work here—15 seconds to soften the ice cream and 1 to 2 minutes to toast the coconut.

➡ **ACTIVE: 10 MINUTES;
TOTAL: 10 MINUTES PLUS
2 HOURS FREEZING**

3 pickled lychees, seeded and coarsely chopped, plus 2 tablespoons (28 ml) strained brine, divided

1 pint (285 g) coconut ice cream, softened

¼ cup (20 g) coconut flakes, toasted

¼ cup (34 g) coarsely chopped macadamia nuts

In a medium bowl, working quickly, fold the lychees into the ice cream. Return the ice cream to the container and freeze until firm, about 2 hours. Scoop the ice cream into bowls, drizzle with some of the brine, and garnish with the coconut and macadamia nuts.

Green Mango Pickle

ACTIVE: 30 MINUTES; TOTAL: 30 MINUTES PLUS OVERNIGHT

These tart and spicy mango pickles, a South Indian staple, are more condiment than pickle. They're heavily spiced with cumin, chile, fenugreek, mustard, curry leaves, and garlic. They are delicious with curries, roasted meats, rice dishes, and grilled bread. It's traditional to keep the skin on—it adds a perfumed sweetness to the sour mango. Look for mangos that are hard as rocks with bright green skin.

MAKES 1 PINT (475 ML)

½ cup (120 ml) canola oil
1 teaspoon black mustard seeds
1 teaspoon cumin seeds
4 dried Asian chiles, broken
3 whole garlic cloves
12 curry leaves
1½ tablespoons (14 g) ground mustard powder
1½ tablespoons (7 g) cayenne pepper
1 teaspoon ground fenugreek
¼ teaspoon ground turmeric
1 teaspoon kosher salt
1 tablespoon (10 g) grated garlic
1 large green, unripe mango (with skin), cut into ½-inch (1 cm) pieces

1. In a small skillet, heat the oil. Add the mustard seeds, cumin seeds, chiles, garlic cloves, and curry leaves. Cook over medium heat until sizzling, about 4 minutes. Transfer to a large bowl, and let cool to room temperature.

2. Add the mustard powder, cayenne, fenugreek, turmeric, salt, and grated garlic. Stir to form a paste. Add the mango and toss to coat evenly. Transfer to a clean, pint-size (475 ml) jar, cover, and refrigerate overnight.

MAKE AHEAD

THE PICKELS WILL KEEP IN THE REFRIGERATOR FOR 4 WEEKS.

Lime-Chile Pickled Pineapple

→ **ACTIVE: 45 MINUTES; TOTAL: 45 MINUTES PLUS OVERNIGHT**

Super tropical and delicious, golden pineapple, lemongrass, habañero, and kefir lime leaves combine to make a fantastic, refreshing, and versatile fruit pickle. It's equally awesome with sweet or savory dishes.

MAKES 1 QUART (950 ML)

½ ripe, golden pineapple
1 stalk (6 inches, or 9 cm) lemongrass, lightly bruised
5 small kefir lime leaves
½ habañero, seeded and sliced
¾ cup (175 ml) distilled white vinegar
½ cup (120 ml) water
½ cup (100 g) sugar
⅛ teaspoon kosher salt

1. Peel and core the pineapple, and quarter it lengthwise. Cut each strip into ½-inch (1 cm)-thick slices. Place the pineapple, lemongrass, lime leaves, and habañero into a clean, quart-size (950 ml) jar.

2. In a small, nonreactive saucepan, combine the vinegar, water, sugar, and salt. Bring to a boil. Pour the hot brine into the jar, seal, and let cool at room temperature. Refrigerate overnight.

MAKE AHEAD

THE PICKLES WILL KEEP IN THE REFRIGERATOR FOR 2 WEEKS.

✧ serving suggestions: Pickles: a tangy addition to fruit salads, chicken and snow pea stir-fry, grilled fruit kabobs, tangy pineapple upside-down cake, or pineapples foster. Brine: add to seltzer, pour over ice cream, stir into lemonade, add to sangria or other punch, freeze into granita.

Pineapple–Aperol Spritz

When you've eaten all of the juicy, yummy pineapple pickles, use the brine to make this refreshing, fizzy cocktail.

MAKES 1 COCKTAIL

 TOTAL: 5 MINUTES

2 ounces (60 ml) white rum
2 ounces (60 ml) Lime–Chile
   Pickled Pineapple brine, plus
   wedges for garnish
¼ ounce (7 ml) Aperol
2 ounces (60 ml) prosecco
Club soda

In an ice-filled cocktail shaker, combine the rum, pickle brine, and Aperol. Shake vigorously. Strain into an ice-filled Collins glass, and add the prosecco and a splash of soda. Garnish with pineapple and serve.

Pickled Rhubarb with Shallots

MAKES TWO ½ PINTS (475 ML TOTAL)

These tart, tannin-rich pickles are best served with rich, well-marbled meats, such as rib eye or pulled pork.

¼ cup plus 2 tablespoons (88 ml) distilled white vinegar
¾ cup (175 ml) water
¼ cup (50 g) sugar
1 tablespoon (9 g) kosher salt
1 teaspoon whole coriander seeds
1 teaspoon crushed red pepper flakes
1 medium shallot, thinly sliced
8 ounces (225 g) rhubarb, cut into ½ x 3-inch (1 x 7.5 cm) pieces

1. In a small, nonreactive saucepan, combine the vinegar, water, sugar, and salt. Bring to a boil.

2. Divide the coriander seeds, pepper flakes, and shallots between 2 clean, ½-pint (235 ml) jars. Add the rhubarb and cover with the hot brine. Seal and let cool at room temperature. Refrigerate overnight.

MAKE AHEAD

THE PICKELS WILL KEEP IN THE REFRIGERATOR FOR 4 MONTHS.